The Jack Russell Terrier

THE
JACK RUSSELL
TERRIER

Katharine Tottenham

David & Charles
Newton Abbot   London

British Library Cataloguing in Publication Data

Tottenham, Katharine
  The Jack Russell terrier.
  1. Jack Russell terrier
  I. Title
  636.7'55   SF429.J27

  ISBN 0–7153–8156–3

First published 1982
Second impression 1983
Third impression 1984
Fourth impression 1986

Typeset by
Northern Phototypesetting Co. Bolton
and printed in Great Britain
by Redwood Burn Limited Trowbridge
for David & Charles Publishers plc
Brunel House Newton Abbot Devon

Contents

Introduction

Young Jack Russell was in his final year as an undergraduate at Oxford in 1819 when he chanced to meet a milkman accompanied by a terrier bitch. She at once caught his eye and he bought her there and then: her name was Trump and she was to be the foundation of his line of working terriers.

My own long association with these terriers dates back to the early 1930s when I was promised a puppy for my tenth birthday. It was to have been a Sealyham, but a few weeks before the day I was walking in a lane near the Devon fishing village of Appledore when I met a man leading a hound-marked smooth puppy on a length of string. Like the parson before me I fell, and boldly for someone aged nine asked the man if his dog was for sale.

'Tezun't a dog,' he replied.

I was nonplussed by this and inquired what it was if it wasn't a dog.

'Tez a bitch,' he said.

In the course of further conversation I obtained his address and went home to broach the subject of cancelling one pedigree Sealyham and buying a puppy seen on the road. I won in the end and went off, armed with a ten shilling note, to collect my present. I named her Tessa and she was my companion for sixteen years. She founded a small dynasty, based on her first litter by a white-and-tan broken-coated dog, which produced two smooths, one broken-coat and one puppy with a smooth but slightly harsh coat and a line of wiry hair along the back. With hindsight I now realise that this proved the dogs to have been of

7

the old strain, since many of Russell's terriers had wiry backs. Tessa's descendants lived on with various members of my family until the mid-1960s when the last of them died.

Looking back over nearly fifty years with the breed it appears to be little changed in comparison with many pedigree breeds. Nervousness has seldom been a problem; in fact, I have never met a shy Jack Russell. Taking Tessa as an example, from puppyhood onwards she was expected to go wherever I went and this meant travelling by car, by train to visit relatives in another county and once a week by bus to a nearby town, where she and I spent the afternoon at the cinema; during the summer we went to sea on my father's yacht. There were no vaccines against canine diseases until after World War II, yet Tessa was treated by a vet only once in her life when a misalliance with a spaniel made caesarian birth essential for her survival. Even then, two days later and still swathed in bandages, she escaped to go hunting with one of her older daughters and returned home hours later, muddy but full of *joie de vivre* – to live for another ten years.

This is the sturdy breed that we have inherited and all of us interested in the continuing prosperity of these dogs should help ensure that only the best in every sense are selected for future breeding.

Katharine Tottenham, Devon, 1982

1

Choosing a Jack Russell Terrier

The origin of the Jack Russell, and its close relatives the smooth and wire-haired fox terriers, is not known with any certainty. It seems likely that they are descended from several extinct types, including the broken-coated black-and-tan terrier; the Old English white, the Devonshire terrier, and a wire-haired beagle known as a terrier beagle, which was commonly used for rabbiting in the eighteenth century.

The Jack Russell of today has evolved to become a recognisable type, and this has enabled the Jack Russell Terrier Club of Great Britain to lay down a standard as a guide for breeders and owners of companion dogs alike. Hitherto there had been a good deal of confusion about the breed: the dogs favoured by the Rev John Russell were larger animals with longer legs, and there are still some among an older generation of country people who will not accept the change in conformation which makes the modern terrier such a neat and attractive small dog.

The parson's ideal dog was the same size as a vixen fox (about 14 inches at the shoulder), with strong, straight legs, and a predominantly white, slightly wiry coat. The size allowed the terrier to creep into an earth in the same way as a fox, and the white hair prevented hounds from mistaking the dog for a fox when it emerged from the earth. Since he disliked over-aggressive behaviour as much as timidity, dogs were valued for their temperament as well as for their other assets, and his habit of keeping several favourites as housedogs as well as workers has left a legacy of terriers which are well adapted to life indoors and out.

There is no doubt that the Jack Russell terrier makes an excellent companion dog. Now usually rather smaller than their earlier counterpart, the dogs may have any of three recognised coats, smooth, broken or rough; and good specimens retain all the qualities of the original.

Innate intelligence makes the dogs easy to train and those with good temperaments are gentle and kindly by nature, seldom picking a fight with a strange dog. But, and this is a reservation to be borne in mind, a Jack Russell has a mixed ancestry of brave animals which might have been expected to risk their lives in badger-baiting or pit fights, and so there is a streak of fighting spirit that can be triggered in certain circumstances.

Jealousy can be a major problem if more than one Jack Russell is kept in a household, and so too can some unexpected occurrence which excites the dogs. As an extreme example, during World War II my parents lived in the country with several of these terriers, miles away from any danger of the blitz until a lost enemy aircraft jettisoned its bombs into their orchard, and this set all the dogs fighting each other as a reaction to fright.

Hunting is an instinct in most dogs and a strong one in the Jack Russell, which enjoys nothing better than a walk in the country with opportunities to search along hedgerows for rabbits – or even mice. A single dog is unlikely to go off hunting on its own, but if two or more are kept, or the dog finds a friend in the neighbourhood, then straying on hunting expeditions can be a real problem; it can only be stopped by fencing the garden with dog-proof wire mesh.

A puppy must learn to live with other pets. It will usually strike up a friendly relationship with a cat, but it may be asking too much to expect a terrier to resist pet rabbits or guinea pigs kept in hutches within its reach, so it is sensible to be safe rather than sorry. This is all part of understanding a chosen breed and in no way discredits the Jack Russell; an owner must take account of a dog's natural inclinations, whether it is a terrier, a gundog or whatever, so that it can be trained within its limits and not offered a chance to give way to undesirable instincts.

If a Jack Russell terrier is given loving care from puppyhood and trained on the basis of its anxiety to please, the breed has everything to recommend it to someone looking for a comparatively small, smart companion dog with the ability to adapt to almost any way of life.

Where to buy

There are basic rules to follow in order to select a good puppy. It is important to find a reliable breeder with a home-bred litter, where the mother can be seen and, ideally, the father too. Members of the Jack Russell Terrier Club will have registered stock for sale, which is a safeguard against buying a mongrel; but many owners of companion dogs breed a few litters of genuine purebred puppies without regard to pedigrees, and one of these may be as good.

Although Jack Russell terriers are not recognised as a breed by the Kennel Club, it can sometimes provide information about breeders in various localities, which may help a novice seeking a good puppy.

The alternative, buying from a dealer, is loaded with risk. Growing popularity has meant that Jack Russells are now in the hands of puppy-farmers, who breed litter after litter without discrimination and sell the unfortunate puppies to dealers. Such puppies are liable to chilling and exhaustion while in transit from kennels to kennels, and so are vulnerable to disease. Moreover, their parentage can be suspect. To meet the demand for a long-bodied, short-legged terrier which can be passed off as a Jack Russell, unscrupulous 'farmers' cross fox terriers with dachshunds or corgis, producing caricatures of the real thing, often with weak spines and crooked forelegs.

In order to make money a dealer must have a quick turnover of stock and sell puppies aged about six weeks and just weaned. These are seen in spotlessly clean cages by an unsuspecting buyer, who is assured that all the puppies have been inoculated and is shown a certificate to prove it. Since inoculation against virus disease at this age is almost certainly ineffective, such a certificate is meaningless and, indeed, the injection may have been positively harmful if the animal is incubating some infection.

It is worth noting that crooked legs may not be due to crossbreeding in every case, but might be an inheritance from a type of smooth-haired terrier known in the nineteenth century. These little dogs were bred with short, splayed legs so that they would hunt rabbits out from underbrush at a slow speed, being naturally somewhat crippled, and so allow sportsmen with muzzle-loading guns time to aim and fire. I have not myself seen a dog with this exaggerated fault for many years and it is to be hoped that whatever bloodlines there were have been extinguished.

The puppy to choose

A sensible buyer will take time over choosing the one and only puppy which is going to join the family and, all being well, live for sixteen years or so. The importance of health is obvious: the kennels should be hygienically kept and the puppies' pen clean, with no sign of diarrhoea or loose droppings because this form of disorder is a symptom of all the virus diseases affecting puppies.

After approving the mother's temperament, which should be calm and friendly, and the surroundings in which she and her puppies live, the next stage is to separate the sexes, and that will whittle down the choice to perhaps two or three individuals out of a normal litter of between three and five pups.

Many people prefer a bitch, because for all but six weeks out of twelve months she makes the most devoted companion. Controlling her during her 'season' may be a problem for anyone without a safely fenced garden. She will have her first season, or oestrus, at about the age of six months and then every six months thereafter, and at those times casts all modesty to the winds in her instinctive desire to have puppies of her own.

An adult dog is to some extent a split personality: half devoted to his human family and half obsessed by his prospects of a love-life with neighbouring bitches of all breeds. This may lead him to stray and make a nuisance of himself if he is not properly trained and supervised.

When a decision has been made between a dog or a bitch, the next stage is to find the pick of the litter – the best puppy. If the puppies were born and spent the first few weeks of their lives in the breeder's house, they are likely to have been under closer observation than kennel-bred animals, which makes it worthwhile to ask two questions. First, has the bitch's favourite been noticed? The majority of bitches when lying at rest with sleeping pups will be seen to have one particular puppy snuggled between their forelegs. Time and time again I have found that this individual will turn out to be a good strong dog, presumably because nature guides the mother to favour an offspring with the best prospects.

That observation can be made up to the age of about three weeks. Meanwhile, once the puppies' eyes have opened at the age of about ten days, there will be one little character with the initiative to be first out of the nest. This is often a bitch pup and, if the breeder has made a note of her, she is likely to prove to have good conformation as she grows, with above-average intelligence.

There are two types of puppy to avoid: first, the shy one which lurks in the background, and second, more surprisingly, the boisterous one intent on chewing fingers and clothes. The former is nervous and so liable to become snappy with age, while the latter is probably stupid and destined to grow up as an unmanageable nuisance.

An intelligent puppy is cautiously friendly towards a strange human being, wagging its tail and giving a tentative lick to a hand, until it gains confidence and is willing to be petted and fussed over. All else being equal, such a puppy will become a loving and intelligent companion – if it fails then almost certainly the fault will lie with its owner.

Before concluding a purchase the puppy should be given a

physical examination. It should be plump, but not pot-bellied because this is a sign of roundworm infestation. A healthy skin is soft and pliable, and the bare skin on the belly and on the inside of the thighs must not show angry spots, which may be a prelude to illness. It is worth noting in this context that Jack Russells have spots or splodges of pigment in the skin which are not necessarily related to colour patches in the hair.

During this part of the inspection the scrotum of a dog puppy should be checked to ensure that both testes have descended properly, because if one is retained within the abdominal cavity it might become the site of a cancerous growth in later life. The teeth should be examined to see that they meet correctly and are not 'over-shot' or 'under-shot' – that is, those in the upper or lower jaw do not project. This might seem a minor fault but improper closure of the teeth can mean that the dog is unable to clean them by the normal action of gnawing bones, with the result that tartar and decay may occur as time goes on. A puppy that passes all these tests has a good start in life and every chance of becoming a healthy adult.

2
Managing a Puppy

The first few days in its new home are bound to be difficult for a puppy which has to become accustomed to unfamiliar sights, sounds, and smells, strange people and the loss of its mother and litter mates. If a new owner can gloss over the strangeness, giving the puppy a sense of security, then it will be easier for it to settle down and enjoy life. The essentials are a bed in a warm but not stuffy place, regular nourishing and appetising meals, suitable playthings and plenty of love and attention.

Sleep is important: given the opportunity a puppy will spend two-thirds of its time asleep and the remaining third exploring and playing. This way of life is natural to a growing animal which is in the process of cell-division to produce growth and learning to use its body and mind by means of play. Rest encourages the body to absorb nutrients for growth, whereas too much exercise will mean that these are used up in providing energy.

Equipment

An indoor pen is very useful for a small puppy. These may be bought complete as four wire-mesh panels which clip together, or a handyman can make one with a wooden framework and sheets of Weldmesh or Twilweld – if this is made in separate panels with two hooks and eyes at each corner for attachment, it can be folded flat for storing. A suitable height for a Jack Russell puppy would be about 30 inches. A puppy pen is used in the same way as a child's playpen, keeping the occupant out of mischief and danger but not isolated from the family.

When choosing a bed for a puppy, do not buy a basket because it will be rapidly demolished by chewing. Plastic beds, either round or oblong, are best as, while not entirely teeth-proof, they generally last for years and can be washed at intervals. Cushions are sold to fit various shapes and sizes of bed, but are a waste of money until a puppy has grown out of the tearing-up stage. Instead, a piece of old carpet cut exactly to fit the bed, with no tempting edges to chew, will make a warm base with a piece of blanket on top.

Cheap grey blankets can be obtained from army surplus stores and these are ideal for dogs. A blanket of normal single-bed size will cut up into four pieces to suit a terrier's bed, and this number

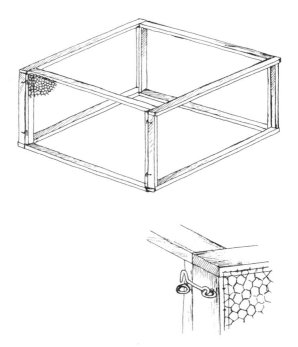

Collapsible puppy pen – wire mesh panels on timber framework, joined together by hooks and eyes at each corner to make square or rectangular enclosure. Height roughly half length/width

The modern smooth-coated Jack Russell terrier

A promising pair of puppies, showing broken and rough-coated types

Terrier racing – leaving the traps in hot pursuit of a rabbit-skin dummy

will allow for frequent washing and airing of the bedding. This is an important but often neglected aspect of dog care: clean bedding means a clean dog because the animal rubs off natural oils from its coat on to its blanket which becomes rancid and makes both the dog and its bed smell.

As an example, I own a fourteen-year-old rough-coated Jack Russell which is white except for a brown eye-patch. Her hair is shining white and people often comment that I must give her a lot of baths, but in fact she has had perhaps half a dozen in her life and then only because she has rolled on some unimaginable filth joyfully discovered in the course of a walk. A comparatively new form of blanket is available for dogs, made from polyester fur fabric. This cannot be torn up, is warm and machine-washable. The only disadvantage is the price, which is high when compared with an army blanket.

It is natural for puppies to be destructive and Jack Russells are no exception: tearing is an instinct and, like most kinds of play, a means of learning – in this case an unnecessary lesson for a domesticated dog which will not have to tear its food from the carcass of its prey, but it is not a good idea to suppress this stage of development; it is part of the 'get up and go' character of a terrier. This is where toys are useful: given an outlet for the tearing instinct, a sensible puppy will soon learn that books, shoes, and cushions are not for demolition but that he can play with various items provided for the purpose.

Empty breakfast-cereal packets make excellent toys, and so do small cardboard cartons, all of which can be ripped in pieces with satisfying noise. A ball of tennis-ball size made of really hard rubber (so that potentially dangerous bits cannot be chewed off and swallowed) is another good plaything; and so is a rawhide chew, sold by most pet shops, if used in moderation – some vets believe that too much rawhide chewing can lead to the development of bladder stones.

Bones are of value: a bone not only occupies a puppy but aids teething and digestive processes. However, it must be of only one sort and that is a beef shin-bone, otherwise known as a marrow bone, which should be sawn to a length of about 4 inches. A puppy can chew this to his heart's content, gradually extracting the marrow, without any danger from splinters. No other bone should be given to dogs, because bones which are likely to splinter, such as chops and vertebrae, can easily result in piercing of the digestive tract, leading to peritonitis and probable death. Fish and poultry bones are also dangerous and must not be given to dogs. The first night alone in his new home is the most traumatic for a puppy, but chewing a juicy shin bone will lull him to sleep and go a long way towards preventing the sorrowful whimpering which so often keeps the whole family awake.

A collar and lead are the next considerations. A Jack Russell puppy needs a light, soft leather collar, and should learn to wear it as soon as he arrives. To begin with he will find it bothersome and tend to scratch, but he soon becomes accustomed to the feel of it. Learning to accept the restriction of a lead may take longer and needs sympathetic training, especially with some individuals who tend to fight this form of control and panic if they are dragged.

The first stage is to attach the lead to the collar and allow the puppy to trail it loose, while he is being supervised so that it does not become entangled. When he is used to this, pick up the end of the lead and follow behind, keeping it slack. Then apply gentle pressure and call him in, shortening the lead as he comes, giving him praise and encouragement all the time. Careful early lead training prevents the tiresome habit of pulling, a common fault in adult dogs.

In recent years choke chains have become popular with owners, if not with their dogs. This device may be useful in the training of a wilful dog of a large breed which has been allowed to get out of hand, but it has no place round the throat of a small breed such as a Jack Russell, which is highly intelligent and quite capable of learning to behave properly without being half throttled in the process.

As a puppy grows to adult size it will need a larger collar, and if its home is in the country and there is a risk of lone hunting expeditions, it is wise to ask a saddler to make a special collar by inserting a 2 inch strip of strong elastic which will allow it to stretch (as is done in cat collars). This will mean that if the collar is snagged in any way, a dog will be able to pull free rather than strangle itself. The collar should have a plate or medallion attached, engraved with the owner's name and telephone number. Never put the name of the dog on its collar as this helps a thief; a dog is more likely to go with a stranger who knows its name.

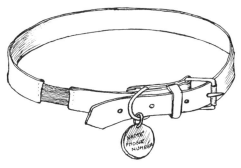

Collar showing elastic inset, about 2in (5cm), and identity disc

House training

The inner workings of a puppy are like a factory, building up the framework of an adult dog, using solid and liquid foods as material and eliminating large quantities of waste products. Thus, while a full-grown dog will empty its bowels once or twice in twenty-four hours, a puppy will do so at least three times as often. The same applies to its bladder, which is a container for excess amounts of water from which nutrients have been extracted – for example, cows' milk consists of 97 per cent water.

With these facts in mind, it is easier to understand why a mismanaged puppy will constantly make 'mistakes' and be difficult to house train. It is hopeless to expect a young puppy to control this output to suit human expectations of behaviour. Initial house training involves realising a puppy's needs and making sure that it is in the right place when its body has to excrete faeces or urine, because up to the age of about ten weeks it appears to have no prior warning of urination but suddenly squats; it does, however, get some message about an impending bowel movement, which makes it trot about in an urgent manner before it relieves itself, allowing the owner time to take it out of doors.

Judging when a puppy will urinate is a matter of timing, combined with taking note of what the animal is doing. Asleep it is safe enough, but the moment it wakes it must be taken out; the same applies immediately after food, whether this is a liquid or solid meal; and in the course of a playtime, since physical activity affects the bladder.

Clearly the early stages of house training involve a lot of care, but it will soon pay off with an intelligent puppy such as a Jack Russell. The principle to work on is that mistakes are the owner's fault, not the puppy's, it cannot know that a carpet should not be used in the same way as grass until it has been taught this fact. Smacking a puppy and rubbing its nose on the dirtied patch serves only to frighten and bewilder it. A dog is a naturally clean animal and a litter of puppies will leave the nest to relieve themselves as soon as they are able to toddle; house training is just a matter of reinforcing the dog's instinct that out of doors is the right place, and a puppy will soon stand by the door to indicate its need to go out.

Night-time presents a problem. A young puppy cannot last through eight hours or so without relieving itself, and the only answer is newspaper laid on the floor, perhaps with a sheet of plastic laid underneath. The use of newspaper as an alternative to out of doors is controversial: many dog breeders are against the practice and insist on a total ban indoors, but I believe that a dog of any age should be allowed as a last resort to use papers spread in a certain place. I have two reasons for this belief: first, if a dog is left at home and the owner's return is delayed, an animal disciplined to absolute cleanness in the house can suffer misery, and, furthermore, it seems probable that enforced retention can lead to diseases of the urinary tract which are common in older dogs. My second reason is connected with weather. To offer a brief example, on one occasion severe winter snow was 3 feet deep, with deeper drifting, around my house for over a week. My elderly Jack Russell bitch, who measures 10 inches at the shoulder, would have presented a problem had she not known that when she could not be let out she could use paper spread on the stone floor of the scullery.

It is useful to train a puppy to respond to some form of command when it is put out for a purpose and 'hurry up' is the most common. But whatever is said the performance must be met with praise: 'good dog . . . clever dog' and so on, while it is brought indoors at once. This practice soon triggers a response, as the puppy learns that it will receive praise and a quick return indoors if it relieves itself promptly.

Introduction to other animals

An established cat may strongly resent having a puppy introduced into its home and so a first meeting should be supervised. Left to itself, a puppy which makes innocent advances to a cat may be badly scratched and even lose an eye, and terriers being what they are, this can make it anti-cat for life. Some years ago I had a pair of Jack Russells which killed a neighbour's cat and, naturally, this put an end to any neighbourly feelings the owner may have had. On the other hand, a tactful introduction, making sure that the cat has no grounds for jealousy, will allow the animals to sort out some sort of relationship: either aloof mutual respect or friendship.

Poultry are a problem and a puppy must learn from an early age that birds must be left alone. The best teacher is a broody hen intent on defending her chicks, as her maternal instinct transforms her into a veritable battleship and one brush with a bird in this frame of mind puts a puppy off fowls for ever. The alternative is to take a puppy on a lead amongst poultry while they are fed: the birds will appear the size of ostriches to a small puppy. If it shows any signs of aggression a sharp tug on its lead and a firm 'No' will put a stop to it after a few sessions.

Jack Russell terriers seldom take to sheep-chasing on their own because that type of hunting is not in their inherited makeup, but one that joins a bigger dog on a foray over farmland can be led into bad ways. There is no doubt, from a dog's point of view, that chasing sheep is great fun and once the game is learned it is very difficult to achieve a cure. Taking a young dog round the sheep pens at a local market can get it used to the sight and smell of these animals before it has a chance to meet them in the open.

Travel

A bought puppy will have its first experience of travelling by car when it is fetched to its new home, which is not the best introduction as the journey is likely to have left alarming memories – although some puppies take to cars like a duck to water. Assuming that it is liable to be nervous, the best way to accustom a puppy to the noise, movement, and sights involved in car travel is to take it in stages. Begin by sitting at the wheel holding the puppy and reassuring it; then, still chatting, start the engine and leave it running for a while. A passenger can now hold the animal while the car is driven slowly for a short distance. In this way, nothing frightening has occurred, and the puppy learns to enjoy outings in the car.

Carsickness affects some puppies. This may be the result of nerves because the animal has not been given a chance to accept this form of travel by degrees, but some people think it appears to be due to static electricity within the vehicles, which can be earthed by attaching a chain to the chassis. Most car-sick dogs (or children) recover as they become used to travelling, but in the meantime a wire-mesh dog crate will keep the puppy and its vomit in one place rather than dirtying the whole car and its occupants. A mild sedative may be effective, but should be given only on the advice of a vet who will prescribe a suitable drug and the correct dosage.

Vaccination

Puppies should be vaccinated against distemper and hardpad, hepatitis and leptospirosis, all of which are contagious killer diseases in dogs. This is done with two simple inoculations given about fourteen days apart. There are two important points to remember about this protective measure: first, the puppy must have been completely weaned from its dam's milk at least four weeks before the injection, because her milk contains antibodies to protect the litter from germs and these antibodies can nullify a vaccine given too soon; and second, until a clear week after the second injection a puppy must be kept away from all contact with strange dogs and, because leptospirosis is also rat-borne, from anywhere likely to be frequented by rats. Avoiding all contact with strange dogs means not only the dogs themselves but any ground outside the garden, because these diseases are transmitted from dog to dog, from faeces and urine, and from nasal and eye discharges. A clear week is necessary to ensure that the vaccine has had time to become effective.

A new disease, canine parvovirus, arrived in Britain in the autumn of 1978 and has been the cause of considerable concern since. Before that time it had been known in the USA and Australia. It is believed to be a type of contagious feline enteritis which formerly did not affect dogs but now attacks both adults and puppies and is extremely virulent. Puppy owners should discuss preventive measures with their vet, who will have up-to-date information on the progress of research and available vaccines against the disease.

Worming

As a general rule, roundworms affect puppies and tapeworms affect adult dogs. A puppy bought from a reliable breeder will have been treated against roundworms at about six weeks of age but the new owner should check that this has been done. A further dose should be given at about twelve weeks unless a puppy shows signs of infestation by passing or vomiting live worms (which resemble short lengths of white string, often curled or entangled), or by its physical appearance – looking thin with a pot-belly and staring coat – though these severe symptoms will have been apparent on the day of purchase and the puppy ought not to have been bought in the first place.

Several proprietary brands of roundworm treatment, based on the drug Piperazine citrate, are obtainable from chemists and pet stores. Some are offered in a flavoured cream which makes dosing simpler.

Tapeworms seldom infest puppies under six months old. This parasite is easily recognised if it appears in faeces or adhering to hairs near the puppy's tail: it is whitish and flat and usually expelled in segments about a quarter of an inch in length. It is commonly picked up by dogs exercised in fields grazed by sheep or wild rabbits. Under the age of six months a puppy should be treated by a vet; over that age it may be dosed with a proprietory tapeworm treatment based on the drug Dichlorophen. Both drugs are safe and effective and do not involve starving the dog beforehand. However, it is important to use the correct dosage which is related to the weight of an animal. The subject of parasitic worms is covered in detail in Chapter 9.

Handling puppies

A Jack Russell puppy should not be picked up and carried except when absolutely necessary, and then it must be handled properly in order to avoid various mishaps. A puppy can squirm like an eel and is easily dropped and injured unless it is held correctly; it should be held by the scruff with the right hand while its rear end is supported by the bent lower left arm and hand. It is secure and comfortable in this position.

Many people tuck a puppy's hind-quarters under an arm with its chest between the forelegs resting on the hand. This is wrong because the puppy can wriggle forwards and fall, and constant handling in this way can give it a crooked front, known by the self-explanatory term 'out at elbows'.

There are other side effects, too. A puppy which is carried about in rain or a cold wind is liable to chilling, especially around the stomach area where the skin is bare and thin. And lastly, picking up leads to the tiresome habit of jumping up, which is difficult to cure. In order to stroke and fondle a puppy it is better

The right way to carry a terrier – left hand and lower arm supporting the dog's rear while the scruff is held in the right hand

The wrong way to carry a terrier – the dog is held under the left arm, supported only by the left hand on its chest between front legs

to kneel or squat down to its level: bending down towards it encourages it to jump up to meet the caressing hand halfway.

Exercise

It is a mistake to take a puppy for walks before it is six months old. Playing in the garden or adjoining paddock is one thing and going for a walk is quite another; at home it can trot off to its bed whenever it is tired, but out on a walk the puppy has to get itself home before it can rest. Exercise on a lead also tends to make the legs grow disproportionately long, weakening the animal's structure and spoiling its conformation.

This does not mean that it should live a cloistered existence; it must become accustomed to the noise and bustle of modern life to avoid later nervousness. But all this is best heard and seen from inside a car until the puppy is old enough for walks. In the meantime, it can of course accompany the family on picnics and other such outings, using the car as a base for rest and sleep when necessary.

Grooming

A Jack Russell's coat needs little grooming apart from an occasional brush to remove dust and loose hairs. A comb should not be used as it is unnecessary for this type of hair and may scratch and inflame the skin.

Various specially prepared grooming powders are obtainable from pet shops and these are useful for cleaning a coat which has become discoloured with earth. The powder is rubbed into the hair and then thoroughly brushed out to remove it and the dirt together. Grooming powder should be used in moderation as it has a drying effect which can make the hair brittle.

As I have mentioned earlier, a well-kept dog seldom needs a bath except when it comes home smelling to high heaven of some filth in which it has rolled. As a rule the stinking patch is found on the shoulders and neck or under one or both ears, and, rather than give the dog a complete bath, this can be simply removed by wetting the area, rubbing it with plain soap to make a lather (do not use detergent as a dog's skin is too sensitive for this type of cleaner), and then brushing, not too hard, with an old nailbrush or scrubbing-brush. The soap must be rinsed out and the area carefully dried.

When bathing a dog, whether wholly or partially, the water should be lukewarm, tested on a wrist or elbow as for a baby's bath. Use a rough towel for drying and keep the animal from becoming chilled while the coat is still damp. The importance of drying a wet dog cannot be over-emphasised. Far too many develop rheumatism or arthritis and become old before their time solely because their owners left them soaked and shivering after a walk in the rain or a swim. A conscientious groom would never stable a wet horse without rubbing it down and providing a warming feed, yet there appears to be a school of thought which suggests that towelling a dog will make it 'soft'. This is ridiculous.

Avoiding accidents

Puppies, in common with young children, are prone to accidents in the home. A distraught owner will exclaim, 'I never imagined it would—' jump out of a window, fall through the banisters, get slammed in a banged door, chew an electric flex, swallow a packet of needles, or whatever the disaster may have been. The answer is that puppies will chew almost anything and many of them appear to believe that they can fly. In my own home, where there is usually at least one puppy among the resident grown-up dogs, the banisters are lined with a form of white plastic mesh designed for supporting climbing plants; the sash windows are opened only at the top; every door which may be blown shut by a draught has a heavy doorstop beside it; and when I am out, every electric appliance is switched off at the wall socket. Potentially dangerous medicines and chemicals are shut away in cupboards or drawers, and so are pins, needles, tacks and the like.

A garden is equally dangerous because puppies (and dogs) can be killed by slug pellets and a variety of insecticides and weedkillers. It is probable that many more dogs are killed by some home hazard than die in traffic accidents. Without becoming obsessed with worry about what might happen, it is sensible to take precautions against avoidable accidents.

Rolling

Those who study animal behaviour have yet to discover why dogs of all ages are attracted to evil-smelling carrion and other substances which they smear on themselves by means of rolling. Some breeds are more prone than others to indulge in this horrid habit and Jack Russell terriers are among the worst offenders. The rotting carcases of animals and birds are popular but a terrier is also likely to roll on fox droppings which have an acrid, pervasive stink. A fox's smell is produced by its anal glands for the purpose of territorial marking, and it may be that domestic dogs roll in order to reinforce their otherwise limited ability to demarcate territory by scent.

Whatever the reason, it is instinctive behaviour and must be accepted as such by a disgusted owner. It is both unkind and a waste of time to be cross with a puppy or dog that has rolled.

3
Feeding Dogs and Puppies

Food is important to a dog for two reasons. We all know that a badly fed animal will not thrive, but what is often forgotten is that feeding time is a highlight in a dog's day, and it gains great pleasure from an appetising meal which has been prepared with imagination and some day-to-day variation in flavour.

Dogs, in common with most animals, are creatures of habit and benefit both mentally and physically from regular meals given at a certain time. The prospect is exciting for them and promotes an expectation in the body, releasing saliva and 'gastric juices' which will aid proper digestion. On the other side of the coin, an owner who feeds the dog at any time when there is a moment to spare has an animal which is prey to a nagging doubt as to whether it will be fed at all, and this in turn leads to begging for titbits and even stealing when it has a chance.

In nature a wild dog hunts, kills, eats and then sleeps. The average domestic dog is required to keep the same hours as its owner, active by day and asleep at night, and this means that it should be fed in the evening – say, within an hour either side of 5 pm at a chosen time that fits in with the household routine. Once a certain time has been established it should be met without fail.

How much food an adult dog needs depends on what sort of life it leads. A companion dog which spends much of the day in and around the house, with its main exercise perhaps an hour's walk, will need less food to maintain itself than a dog used for sport. The diet of a domestic dog consists of protein and carbohydrates in the form of animal products and wholemeal

31

biscuits. In basic terms, protein is used to build up muscle and renew wear and tear in the body tissues. If a dog receives too little protein it will draw on reserves in its muscles and fail to thrive; if it receives too much, on the other hand, there is strain on the kidneys, and excess in the intestines can cause toxic substances to be absorbed into the blood stream.

The digestive processes are geared to absorbing protein from animal sources, and so vegetable protein, obtained from plants such as beans, although valuable in the diet of a human being, are of little if any use to a dog.

Carbohydrates may be considered as fuel, producing heat and energy. Any excess is laid down as fat in various parts of the body and in reasonable amounts acts as a reserve. Too much fat is undesirable as it can lead to diverse ills, including heart trouble.

It is sometimes difficult for a novice owner to decide whether a dog is too fat or too thin because the average person has little knowledge of how muscles relate to the skeletal structure of an animal, except in terms of a butcher's beast which has been developed to produce an unnatural amount of meat (muscle).

In this case, the skinned carcass of a wild rabbit offers a useful example. A rabbit in good condition will have a thick layer of meat all along the spine from the head to the root of the tail, leaving no sign of the vertebrae beneath; the shoulders, too, are well muscled and the hind legs even more so – the thighs shaped like breeches; the ribs are covered in thin layers of muscle, just concealing the underlying bones.

Bearing in mind that a Jack Russell is naturally stockily built with strong bone, it is possible to run the hands over the dog, and using the rabbit as a guide, feel the muscles lying under its skin. If the vertebrae and hip-bones protrude it is too thin, but if the rib cage cannot be felt this is probably hidden under a layer of fat.

The basic diet of a dog is meat and biscuits moistened with stock, gravy or milk; the solids in a ratio of one part meat to two parts biscuit. An adult Jack Russell terrier will need about two generous handfuls of biscuit meal to the equivalent of a quarter of a large tin of dog meat (approximately $3\frac{1}{2}$ oz), the actual amount depending on the dog's size and weight and whether its condition suggests a need for more nourishment or less.

To buy cheap dog foods can be false economy. This particularly applies to biscuit meal: an expensive meal sold under a known brand name is likely to be good meal, whereas bulk supplies of unbranded so-called 'terrier meal' may be made with inferior flour which can cause gastric upsets.

Another source which can be suspect is knacker's meat, that is meat obtained from a slaughterer specialising in old horses and casualty farm animals. According to British law this meat must be steam cooked at a high temperature before sale, which means that much of the goodness is destroyed. And while an old horse, put down for no reason other than infirmity, produces healthy meat, the same cannot be said of farm animals which may have died of disease after being dosed with unknown quantities of drugs. Either way, this sort of meat is not good food for a dog.

A butcher can supply various kinds of meat and offal suitable for dogs.

Beef: shin and skirt are cheaper cuts which can be fed raw; minced or cut small for puppies and cubed for dogs.

Ox Liver: this must be cooked, except for small amounts which may be chopped and fed raw mixed with other foods – too much raw liver induces vomiting. This is a valuable food but should be given in moderation – say once a week, using the stock to moisten the meal.

Heart: ox, sheep, or pigs' hearts are enjoyed as a change. However, the meat tends to be somewhat indigestible, which makes it unsuitable for puppies or elderly dogs.

Udder: boiled cow's udder makes an excellent meal. It often contains some milk which makes a nice stock. Most butchers will obtain udder on request or it may be had direct from an abattoir.

Lamb's head: this must be complete with brains and tongue to provide several varied meals and stock. The head should be sawn, not chopped, lengthways (chopping can leave splinters hidden in the meat). It will need boiling for some time so that the meat falls off the bone.

'Melt': this is the butcher's name for a sheep's spleen, an organ

33

connected with the blood supply. Dogs will not eat it raw but find it very palatable when boiled and served in its own juices.

Paunch: raw paunches are available only from an abattoir, usually by arrangement with some helpful employee. It is the stomach of a sheep and resembles a piece of dirty-green bath-towel; it should be boiled. Cooking paunches is not an occupation for the squeamish as the resultant smell can only be described as a stench, but it makes a cheap, nourishing and appetising meal for a dog.

Lights: the butcher's name for sheep's lungs. This has no food value and should not be used.

Pigs' trotters: these are pigs' feet which, when thoroughly boiled, produce some meat and a stock which cools to a jelly. Quite a good food, offering a change in flavour, particularly in hot weather when a dog may like a cold meal.

Rabbit: a rabbit should be boiled and the meat carefully removed from the bones (even the smallest bone can be dangerous if eaten). The liver and kidneys may be used to make a separate meal.

Giblets: some butchers sell the edible offal from poultry separately, under the English term giblets. They are from chicken, turkey or duck and consist of the liver, kidneys, neck and gizzard. The gizzard must be cut open and cleaned of its contents of grit and fibrous matter before cooking. Stewed giblets, with the meat stripped from neck vertebrae, are appetising and of reasonably good feeding value when given with the stock.

Most dogs enjoy boiled fish for a change. It should be white-fleshed because the dark kinds such as herring suppress other nutrients in a dog's food. Careful boning is essential, which cuts out very bony species like whiting. Among cheaper fish, coley fillets are good and it is sometimes possible to obtain dogfish, which can be cut in 'steaks' for cooking.

As mentioned earlier, eggs are of great value and at least one or two should be given raw every week. Duck eggs are often cheaper than hens' eggs, but a poultry farm may have slightly cracked eggs available on the basis of a standing order.

A working terrier out with the hunt (*The Beaford Archives*)

Pixies Puffin of Freedom at Turners Hill terrier races

Under the judge's eye are displayed all the qualities of a champion Jack Russell terrier – keen but kindly expression, straight front, muscular body and well angled hind legs

Dogs like cheese of the cheddar type and it can be given occasionally, shredded over a prepared meal. A friendly grocer may have crumbled pieces or rind to spare.

Milk is good for dogs of all ages, cold or slightly warmed in winter. There is an old wives' tale that milk gives dogs worms: this is nonsense. Untreated milk which has gone sour in curds is enjoyed by most dogs and is nourishing for adults but unsuitable for puppies. Treated, so-called long-life milk that has gone off should not be given as it goes bad rather than sour.

Vegetables

Some years ago I owned two species of wild dog: a female dingo and a pair of a small Asian species known as racoon-like dogs. Caring for them made me realise how much dogs like, and apparently need, vegetables in their diet, because all three ate raw cabbage, lettuce and carrots with gusto, and also enjoyed fruit. Since then I have always given my domestic dogs some vegetables in their diet – either raw or cooked, depending on the time of year.

Cabbage of various kinds, including kale and Brussels sprouts, is best boiled and given with the water in which it was cooked; raw lettuce should be chopped fine and mixed with the meal; carrots may be given raw as a chew or grated or boiled.

Vegetables have a secondary use in the case of greedy dogs tending towards obesity: they provide bulk to satisfy their hunger but without any fattening results.

Convenience foods

Most owners rely to some extent on packaged and canned foods which are now available in numerous varieties to suit dogs of all ages. As with human foods, you get what you pay for: cheaper products are likely to contain higher proportions of cereal and vegetable protein instead of meat protein.

Reputable manufacturers spend a lot of time and money on the development of dog foods, maintaining their own kennels where the foods are tested before marketing. These firms have developed dry complete feeds in pellets or flake form which require only the addition of water, milk or stock to make a palatable meal; they also produce various canned meats for general use, and several special diets to suit puppies, elderly dogs and those inclined to obesity.

Products of these kinds sold under known brand names are all good in their way, either as standby feeds or as a major part of a dog's diet, but (in my opinion) cannot replace fresh foods for nourishment and tastiness – it is like comparing the traditional English Sunday lunch of roast beef and vegetables with cans of corned beef and baked beans!

Freezing dog foods

Anyone who owns a freezer can economise by making up varied stews and freezing these in bags containing enough for one or two meals. All kinds of butcher's meat are suitable but I would hesitate to store bagged paunch among food intended for human consumption.

Feeding elderly dogs

While the Jack Russell terrier is normally long lived by comparison with several other breeds, it does benefit from special care as it grows older. Far too many elderly dogs have an unpleasant smell due to gastric disorders or bad teeth, both of which could be avoided in most cases by judicious feeding.

At about nine or ten years old it is better to divide the usual daily amount of food into two meals, one at midday and the other at the usual evening hour. This will avoid overloading the stomach. Foods should be of a light, easily digested nature, including raw meat, milk and eggs (white of egg is particularly beneficial for old dogs with weak hearts).

The dog should be encouraged to gnaw beef shin bones daily because this not only keeps the teeth clean and healthy but promotes salivation which helps digestion.

Feeding a puppy

At the age of eight weeks a puppy needs four meals a day. These are divided into two solid feeds and two milk feeds, which may be conveniently given to coincide with the family's breakfast, lunch, tea and supper.

The first feed should be of milk, or milk and beaten-up raw egg, slightly warmed.

The second should be solid and made up of puppy grade biscuit meal moistened with a good stock.

The third, at teatime, is of milk.

The final feed should be of plain meat, minced or chopped small, and preferably raw.

A teaspoonful of codliver oil and one veterinary yeast tablet should be added to one of the solid feeds in the day. This will provide additional vitamins and minerals for the growing animal.

Remember to put the puppy out immediately after a meal so that it can relieve itself. The reason for giving plain meat as the final feed of the day is to provide the best nourishment through the long night hours, while avoiding too much liquid in the stomach which will be passed to the bladder and from there onto the floor. But the puppy must not be deprived of water overnight as a thirsty animal cannot digest its food properly.

At fourteen weeks old the feeds can be reduced to three: two solid and one liquid, cutting out the teatime milk and giving the last meat meal earlier – say at 8 pm.

At six months old a puppy will need only two meals a day, both solid but, since milk is such a good food for dogs, one feed should be moistened with milk.

When a puppy reaches the age of one year it may be considered an adult and fed accordingly, with one evening meal in the day.

Up to the age of twelve months I believe in taking minute care of a puppy, paying particular attention to its everyday diet and general management, and keeping it a little on the fat side while it is growing. This early care produces a sturdy, disease-resistant dog, which will amply repay all the trouble taken.

Minerals

Calcium and phosphates are the only two minerals which need concern a dog owner. Large breeds with big bones may suffer from mineral deficiency but, as a general rule, a well-fed Jack Russell terrier puppy or dog will not require additional mineral supplements if milk and eggs form part of its diet. There is a widespread belief that excess minerals are excreted by the body, but this is not strictly true and in some cases of over-dosing the result can be stones (calculi) in the urinary tract which can be cured only by surgery. However, a puppy will benefit from limited doses of veterinary yeast tablets, a source of calcium and phosphates and vitamin B, particularly in winter.

Vitamins

Vitamins play an important role in the development of a puppy and the maintenance of an adult dog. The principal vitamins related to dog care are A, B, D and E (vitamin C which is so vital to the health of human beings is not needed by dogs in their diet and it is thought that they are capable of synthesising this substance within their own bodies).

Vitamin A promotes growth in a young animal and renewal in the adult. It is present in egg yolk, liver, milk and codliver oil. A deficiency stunts growth and reduces natural protection against disease.

Vitamin B is important for growth, the nervous system and heart, and in the conversion of carbohydrates. It is present in egg yolk, ox liver, red meat and yeast. A deficiency affects growth and leads to nervous disorders and eczema.

Vitamin D has one main function: acting as a catalyst, aiding the absorption of calcium and phosphate. Sunlight is the major source but it is also present in egg yolk, milk, meat juices and codliver oil. A deficiency can cause rickets.

Vitamin E is often described as the fertility vitamin but recently has been recognised as generally important to well-being. It is present in red meat and in wheat-germ oil. A deficiency can cause sterility in both dogs and bitches.

Clearly, meat, eggs and milk are important in a dog's diet if it is to be kept in good condition. There is also a modern trend towards using 'convenience foods' and proprietary forms of vitamin and mineral additives, which is all very well in moderation but there ought to be a proportion of natural foods in the diet to maintain a healthy dog from puppyhood to old age. Furthermore, a heavy-handed use of mineral and vitamin supplements can have undesirable effects: for example, excess amounts of yeast fed to pigs as a Vitamin B supplement will induce severe rickets.

A sensible owner should use good-quality wholemeal biscuit and add to this a variety of protein foods, including tinned meat and suitable household scraps, to make up balanced and appetising meals.

4
Obedience Training

Basic obedience is necessary so that a Jack Russell, or any other breed of dog for that matter, can live happily and safely with a human family without being a nuisance to other people or a danger in traffic. It involves teaching the dog to be clean in the house, to come promptly when it is called, to walk sensibly on a lead, and to sit or lie down when told.

Lessons should begin as soon as the puppy arrives in its new home at the age of about eight weeks, so that when it is six months old it will be reasonably obedient to simple commands and will relieve itself only in designated places. Obedience training given on the right lines is enjoyable for both the puppy and its owner, as they share a sense of achievement with each lesson learned and performed correctly.

When a puppy has learned its name it will come when called once it has become attached to its owner and expects affection, and of course meals, at regular intervals. It is important to establish a set of words of command which are short and clearly different: 'No' (stop whatever it is doing); 'Sit'; 'Down' (lie down); 'Come' (come here); 'Stay' (remain sitting or lying down); 'Leave' (give up what it is carrying or about to pick up); 'Seek' (search for an object); 'Heel'; and 'Stop'.

The command 'Heel' should be mainly used as an instruction to walk properly on a lead, because there are too many distractions and dangers along most town and country roads to allow a dog to walk freely at heel.

Apart from 'Come', the command 'Sit' is easily learned at an early age if a puppy's hindquarters are gently pressed down to a sitting position and the word is said clearly. Success must be met with warm-voiced praise, as should every other obedient response. Praise, not blame, is the basis of all successful training.

Lead training is another early lesson. Although a puppy will not be taken for walks, it should learn at home to walk on a lead without pulling forward or dragging back. In later life a lead will represent the fun of going out somewhere, but it may be frightening at first to a young puppy, and so it should be introduced carefully, with encouragement and praise. When the puppy has accepted the restraint it can be walked about a room or the garden, always keeping to the left and with the objective of learning to keep level with the owner's knee. This is a foundation lesson for a well-behaved dog, not always easy to instil but once learned seldom forgotten.

At between four and six months of age the other commands can be taught. Training must be taken slowly and patiently, with each phase clearly explained by example and unvaried repetition of the same word each time a command is given. It is not only unnecessary but wrong to shout; a dog's hearing is far more acute than a human's. But clarity is of the essence. A splendid instance of misunderstanding happened when a visitor told one of my dogs, which was making polite overtures, to sit, but pronounced the word like 'seat'. The immediate result was chaos because the dog mistook the word for 'Seek' and proceeded to hurtle round the room hunting for rabbits or rats!

I believe in getting the basic training under way early because in most puppies' lives there comes one stage when they try to see how much disobedience they can get away with, and if training is left till this age, they will be that much more difficult to teach.

Training sessions should be confined to about a quarter of an hour each day; a longer time will bore the animal and result in slovenly work. Always try to end the session with a success, so that the puppy can be congratulated and given a titbit prize. It is an odd fact that a puppy in the initial stages of training seems to mull over what he has been taught and work better the next day.

Some trainers are against using titbits of food as an incentive, but there is no doubt that the prospect of a prize makes a puppy keener at first. When training has progressed to a point where it understands and enjoys the lessons, then titbits can be phased out and replaced by 'Good dog!' which will please it just as much. I use morsels of hard cheese as prizes, because this is clean to handle and good for the dog, whereas sweets or candy are not.

So far I have not explained the final word in my list of suitable commands: 'Stop'. This is the only command to be shouted in a parade-ground voice and it is reserved for emergencies, used alone without any preliminary order. A dog accustomed to listening for commands given in a normal tone will be shocked into instant obedience by a sudden yell, and this will prevent it from crossing a road amongst traffic or joining a fight.

It should be taught as an ultimate lesson when the puppy is nearly adult and fully conversant with the rest of the training programme. A suitable situation can be achieved by taking the puppy to a safe place and allowing it to wander off for some distance. When it is facing ahead and still going away, the single shout is given and this will stop it in its tracks to look back in shocked surprise. Then follows the normal command 'Come', and a joyful greeting when the puppy returns. This lesson is so different from all the others, because of the imperative shout, that it need only be given about twice, with a lapse of time in between, to ensure that a prompt response has been engraved on the puppy's memory.

Some puppies that learned to walk sedately on a lead when they were young begin to pull as they grow older and more self-confident. This is most likely to happen on a known route to some pleasant place, such as a field or park where they are accustomed to free exercise. The habit must be nipped in the bud before it takes hold and turns every walk into something resembling a dog-sled race. A rolled-up newspaper is the best tool for the job; three or four sheets of a large newspaper, tightly rolled and retained by elastic bands, should be used to tap the puppy's nose lightly as it begins to pull; at the same time give the command 'No'! It is important not to use this paper stick in a frightening manner but just as a reminder.

A sturdy puppy already shows strong forelegs and paws designed for digging. This champion-bred example has all the makings of the desirable type of smooth-coated Jack Russell for which breeders are now aiming

This quartet is of the smaller type, similar in conformation but with different coats

A misjudgement of speed has meant that the dummy was caught. The puppy looks on with interest but is wise enough not to interfere

Waiting for the next race

Jack Russell bitches make devoted mothers. Pixie has adopted two Border collies to rear with her own single puppy

The use of choke chains is a post-World War II innovation that seems bad. A puppy can be trained by taking advantage of its natural desire to please and earn praise, and no force is necessary. Rigid discipline may be necessary for army and police dogs, but has no place in the training of a terrier puppy destined to be a household companion. Its lessons are designed to teach it to behave in a sensible manner so that it does what it is told but is also free to enjoy life.

Further training

While further training may be described as an optional extra, Jack Russell terriers are highly intelligent and energetic dogs and need plenty to occupy them both physically and mentally. This makes the breed ideal for anyone who wants a constant companion which will go everywhere with them on foot, or by car or bus: a dog leading this sort of life will be happily employed between times when it is content to sleep in its basket or on the hearthrug. But nowadays it is not always possible to take a dog shopping or to a local pub because more and more places are banning dogs as a matter of policy. (Much of the blame for this situation lies with owners of unruly dogs. In years gone by, several dogs could be seen with their owners in an English village inn, the animals ignoring each other, lying down quietly until it was time to leave.) But since restrictions do exist, other occupations may be needed to keep a young terrier from mischief and straying, and these are all the better if they involve exercise for the dog. Training to 'seek' and to 'stay' are two lessons it will enjoy as they require mental effort and a good deal of activity.

'Seek' is comparatively easy to teach. Some object, say a hard rubber ball, a stuffed rabbit skin or a child's discarded rag doll, is thrown some distance while the dog is held. It is then released with the command 'Seek' and when it has found and picked up the object, is recalled with the known command 'Come'. With a little patience a dog will quickly learn that this is fun and that retrieving means another throw. Until this stage the object, known as a 'dummy' in training circles, has been in full view.

The next stage is to throw it into long grass or undergrowth so that it is harder to find, and the dog will be delighted when it returns in triumph with a trophy that has been discovered after a search. When this has been learned, dummies can be hidden without the dog's knowledge, which means that he must seek on command and respond to directions given by the owner's hand signals. These lessons have a practical application if the dog is used for rabbiting.

'Stay' is a lesson in self-control for the dog, and the word may also be used when an owner is going out somewhere, leaving the dog at home or in the car.

In the field, garden or wherever, the lesson begins with the command 'Sit', which has already been learned at a young age. A simple progression for this is 'Down': the dog is gently pressed so that it is lying down, facing forwards. This stage needs endless patience and plenty of praise while the owner stands in front with a hand raised. When the dog is steady, retreat backwards repeating the command 'Stay' in a firm but kindly voice.

Inevitably, the dog will try to follow and each time it must be returned to the same spot, with the performance repeated all over again until it understands what it is meant to do. Again, patience is the watchword. When it has stayed where it has been placed while the owner has taken about a dozen steps backwards, the hand should be lowered and the dog recalled with the command 'Come'. The reunion must be joyful, with much praise and petting. In due course, with careful training, a dog will learn to stay while the owner walks away for a hundred yards or more. It can be seen quivering as it controls itself in anticipation of the recall, and this is good for it mentally, while the dash on recall provides exercise.

An important point to remember is that training and the performance of learned lessons must not be overdone. A dog will become bored and indeed worn out by constant tests of its training, so that what had been fun and a source of pride becomes nothing more than a dreary circus act.

I have found that Jack Russell terriers are mentally adult at the age of twelve months (which is not true of some other breeds that I have kept, notably Dalmatians and Labradors, which were still puppyish at two years old). At a year old, a sensible terrier will have learned, assuming that it was properly taught, the nine commands I have suggested and several other words besides. One of these is 'walk', which I find tiresome, because the word can be used unthinkingly in the course of conversation with the result that there is an instant turmoil of expectant terriers. In my parents' house, where we had seven Jack Russells, the family were reduced to translating 'walk' into French and then into German, but the dogs learned that too within a very short time, and went on to understand even when the letters were spelled out.

This is an example of how much a dog will listen and learn on its own. An owner is under surveillance all the time, little realising that every unconscious gesture is being duly noted. There is also a varying degree of telepathic communication which I have tested out on walks with my dogs. When they were all trotting ahead, I have concentrated on one in particular and then said, 'What a good little dog!' in a normal voice. The dog in question has wagged and wriggled its backside without looking round to catch my eyes.

Since a dog is listening to every nuance, once it has learned a set of single commands it can be talked to in sentences on a much more friendly basis, such as 'Be a good dog and go and sit in your basket(bed).' It will extract from this the words 'good dog', 'sit' and 'basket', and take the appropriate action.

Teaching tricks

Tricks have gained a bad name in some quarters but I think that, in moderation, a few are much enjoyed by a dog, which likes using its brain and proving how clever it is. One of my terriers, sadly long dead, was an enthusiastic piano player – leaping onto the keyboard to race up and down, making an appalling noise and doing little good to the instrument. She would also shut a door when asked – which was more useful, except that it was given a window-rattling slam.

Another bitch pretended to be a mathematician, barking three times when asked 'What is the square root of nine?' In truth, it was the nine that triggered the barks, and the whole performance fell apart if a visitor demanded other examples.

On a more practical level, I have always taught my dogs to jump over my arm. This can be a very useful trick on a country walk when the way is barred by a fence (not that I am promoting trespass), because then a dog will jump a sleeve laid along the top of the obstacle and so avoid barbed wire or other possible injury.

Extra lessons for town dogs

A dog living in a town must be taught to relieve itself at the edge of the road and not on the pavement or sidewalk. This is vital, because the strong anti-dog lobby flourishing in urban and suburban areas has grown up because too many dog owners allow their animals to foul pavements and children's playgrounds. Other more responsible owners suffer from the behaviour of these irresponsible people, finding that dogs are banned from public parks and other places where they can be safely exercised.

Gutter training is simply a stage beyond house training. The dog is led to the edge of the pavement to pass its excreta and soon learns to do this on its own accord. It is now possible to buy a hygiene kit consisting of a small plastic shovel and disposable bags, which can be used when the dog is exercised in open spaces.

Training classes

There are some novice dog owners who find difficulty in teaching animals how to behave properly. This is often due to a lack of confidence, both in themselves and in a dog's willingness to learn: they ask for obedience rather than ordering it, and a lively and intelligent young dog soon realises this and takes advantage of a lack of control in much the same way as a spoiled child. Yet neither the dog nor the child is happier for this freedom.

Local training classes have been established in many countries in order to meet this problem. These groups usually meet once a week for evening sessions over a period of three months or so, and particulars may be obtained from a town hall or mayor's office or from a dog breeder in the neighbourhood. As a rule there is a small enrolment fee to cover costs.

A class is in the charge of a qualified instructor. This person may be a local breeder who specialises in obedience with working dogs of one sort or another. A good instructor sums up the people attending the class, not their dogs and then uses a three-tier system of teaching. The first stage is to teach each owner how to give orders and expect them to be obeyed, which is the very foundation of obedience training.

This requires considerable understanding on the instructor's part, because it is difficult for a trainer to realise that some owners have no rapport whatsoever with their own dogs. I remember visiting a lady whose large dog was being a considerable nuisance to me, sniffing and jumping up. She apologised, telling me that only her husband could keep the animal under any control. Normally, I am loath to give an order to someone else's dog, but as things were getting out of hand, I locked eyes with this one and said 'Sit'. It gave me an amazed glance and sat, and then was no problem. The owner went on about what a way with animals I must have, when in fact all I did was to convince the dog that I expected obedience.

An instructor has to instil this conviction in his, or her, human pupils, because the principle behind training classes is to teach the owners how to teach, which means that they must accept being given a hard time during one or two of the early sessions.

The next stage is to tell the owner what order the dog is to be given and see that this message is passed on firmly and correctly so that the dog obeys. Most owners gain enormous benefit from these classes if they are willing to submit to this kind of regimentation, finding that they have achieved a different relationship with their dogs, which is happier for human and animal alike.

I must add, however, that I am no admirer of the type of obedience practised in shows where a dog is required virtually to glue itself to the trainer's left leg, marching about like a recruit under orders from a drill sergeant. I have never seen a Jack Russell terrier entered in such a class and hope I never will.

Preventing gunshyness

If a puppy is to work with guns when it is grown up then it must learn at an early age not to fear the sound of gunfire. Apart from a few with super-sensitive hearing, the majority of gunshy dogs are afraid because they have been introduced to shooting in the wrong way.

At one time I bred and trained as gundogs labradors, pointers, and cocker spaniels, and had an unfailing method of introducing them to shot at the age of about ten weeks. Then, as now, even blank cartridges were expensive, and so in the initial stages a gun was replaced by paper bags. A helper is needed for the first lessons so that the owner can concentrate on the puppy, which is taken out on to the house lawn or to a nearby field and, most importantly, held on a lead to prevent it from running away if it is accidentally scared.

The helper stands some distance away, say the length of a tennis court, and blows up one of the bags, while the owner holds the puppy and directs its attention so that it is looking towards the sound of the burst when this happens. An owner should talk to the puppy in a cheerful eager voice; implying that something exciting is in the wind – 'Good dog, clever dog, watch now!' – and then signals for the burst.

Bursting a paper bag is a minor art but, properly done, the result is remarkably like the sound of a shotgun. A puppy may flinch but is soon reassured with petting and the suggestion that this is a jolly occasion, not a frightening one. Restrict the explosions to not more than three on the first day, the helper approaching a little nearer each time. This training is best included in a short obedience session so that it becomes part of everyday learning. Assuming that a puppy is not subject to hearing problems, it will accept the sound of gunfire after the first day and soon reaches a point where the owner can burst bags while standing beside it. But this is not a lesson to be hurried, and if there is any sign of nervousness the bangs must be kept at a distance until it has become accustomed to them.

Once the puppy is clearly unafraid, this part of its training can be abandoned as it will not now be gunshy in later life. I have used this method with several Jack Russells and never had a failure with the breed, which works well with a gun shooting 'for the pot' or ferreting.

5

Breeding

The owner of a Jack Russell bitch will be tempted to breed from her. Certainly a bitch benefits from having a litter of puppies because this natural function matures her both physically and mentally, besides giving her the pleasure of motherhood. However, it must be realised that a litter involves the owner in giving a considerable amount of care between mating and the sale of the resultant puppies, a period totalling nearly five months.

Accommodation may be a problem. There must be somewhere quiet and secluded in the house where the bitch can give birth and nurse her puppies for the first two weeks of their lives, secure from disturbance by children or visiting strangers. Then, once their eyes have opened, the puppies will climb out of the nest and begin to toddle about, which means that some form of barricade is needed to keep them within bounds.

While puppies are feeding exclusively on the bitch's milk she will keep them clean, but when they begin to take other foods from the age of about three weeks she will no longer do this, and from then on there is the constant chore of keeping the pen tidy – even a small litter produces a large amount of liquid and solid excreta which must be frequently cleaned up in order to keep the puppies themselves clean.

Over the years I have reared litters in various places, including a horse loose box or box stall, the fenced-off end of a conservatory, and indoors in a puppy pen of the type described in Chapter 2. The advantage of the movable pen is that it can be

Young puppies often have spotted pigment on the nose. This is not a fault, the skin will turn black as the puppy develops. A flesh-coloured nose would be a fault

A typical pair show the alert, intelligent expression of a good Jack Russell (*Panther Photographic International*)

Supreme Champion Tantivy Tess is a keen worker with a pack of foxhounds. The ideal Jack Russell not only wins in the show-ring, but also has the courage and stamina to face a fox underground

put out on a lawn during warm dry weather to give the puppies the benefit of sunshine and fresh air.

Clearly, breeding puppies requires forethought, but if time and accommodation are available it can be interesting and rewarding – though seldom financially so.

The bitch

There is no such animal as a dog that perfectly accords with the official standard, whether it is of a breed recognised by the Kennel Club or a registered Jack Russell terrier. Even champion dogs will have some minor fault, and the art of breeding better dogs involves matching good points against bad ones. This applies equally to temperament: if two bad-tempered dogs are mated, the majority of their offspring are liable to be 'right little hellers'.

This means that the owner of a bitch should look her over with eyes free from rose-tinted spectacles. Glaring faults are readily seen (cow hocks, crooked forelegs, etc) but it is *tendencies* that need looking for: slightly bowed legs, a slight dip in the line of the back, a slightly low-set tail, and so on. These almost unnoticeable faults can be magnified in the puppies if a bitch is mated to a dog with the same tendencies. These factors are all the more important now that the Jack Russell breed is in the process of standardisation under the aegis of the Jack Russell Terrier Club. A novice owner proposing to breed from a bitch would be well advised to attend a show with her where she can be faulted and available stud dogs seen and compared.

When a bitch will come in season is to some extent dependent on the time of year and the weather. Sunny weather in early spring may bring her on, but she may delay if it is cold and wet. A bitch puppy's first season usually occurs when she is between the ages of six and eight months and it is vital that she is kept secure from any chance of meeting a dog at this time, because such early breeding would be very bad for her. Furthermore, a bitch that escapes while in season may well choose an unsuitable mate.

In his book *How To Breed Dogs,* the American veterinary

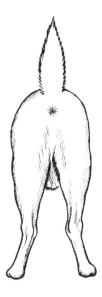

Cow hocks – bent inwards instead of being straight when viewed from the rear

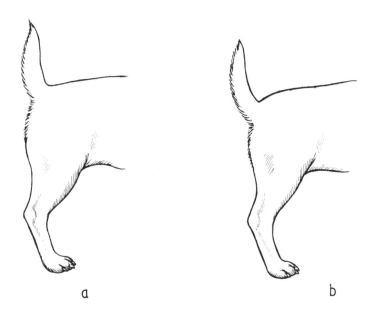

a   b

(a) Tail correctly set; (b) tail set too low

geneticist L. F. Whitney describes a study on which type of dog a bitch will select if she has a free choice from amongst various followers, and the result was that almost invariably she will pick a sheepdog, regardless of what breed she is herself! This conclusion presents a stern warning, because if a Jack Russell bitch were to mate with a dog of collie size she would have to endure a dangerously difficult time giving birth to the puppies, with the probability of a caesarian operation, leaving the owner with an ill bitch, a nondescript mongrel litter and a substantial vet's bill.

In theory, a season lasts for twenty-one days from the first sign, which is the passing of a few droplets of blood. The parts then swell to reach maximum size on about the tenth day and by the twenty-first day have returned almost to normal. But twenty-one days must not be taken as a hard and fast rule. I learned this the hard way years ago, when I let out a bitch at the appointed time, when she had apparently finished her season. After a few weeks she began to get fatter and fatter, and with visions of dropsy or some other dread disease I sent for the vet. He listened with his stethoscope and then turned to me laughing. 'Puppies,' he said. He was right and in due course she had a nice litter, fortunately having gone off with my own dog when no one was looking. Even so, that episode taught me a lesson.

When to plan a mating depends on the time of the first season. If it occurs at six months and again at twelve months, the bitch should be mated in her third season when she will be eighteen months old and physically mature, but with the pelvic bones still pliable enough to allow an easy passage for the puppies as they are born. If the seasons do not occur at the usual intervals, it is a matter of commonsense to time the mating so as to breed from a bitch when she is between one and half and two years old.

The dog

The small breeder who plans an occasional litter from a companion bitch would be sensible not to keep a dog as well. There are two main reasons for this: first, he will be a nuisance when the bitch is in season and not breeding, and second, he will be even more of a problem if bitch puppies are kept from one or more litters, because neither by accident nor by design should one embark on inbreeding Jack Russells.

Inbreeding means breeding between close relatives such as father/daughter, mother/son, or brother/sister. There is no doubt that exhibitors in pedigree breeds have achieved spectacular success by means of expert inbreeding, but I submit that has been to the long-term detriment of those breeds; in too many cases the result has been poor temperaments and the appearance of hereditary malformations and disease.

Line-breeding is another matter and may prove useful in establishing the true Jack Russell type. In basic terms, line-breeding means keeping to certain well-matched families in both the sire and dam's ancestral line, so that for instance they share a common grandsire but have different grand-dams. As time goes on and more and more dogs have qualified for entry in the Jack Russell Terriers Club's advanced register, this sort of breeding will become easier to plan.

Among horse breeders, myself included, it is generally agreed that the sire's dam has a marked effect upon her grandchildren (as anyone looking for a Derby winner might note), and this is worth remembering when choosing a stud dog if his parentage is known.

While his temperament and appearance are of first importance, it is better to use an experienced stud dog on a maiden bitch, and vice-versa.

Mating

When the bitch is due to come in season she should be dosed against tapeworms as a routine measure, and in areas where there have been outbreaks of parvovirus a vet will advise on whether a booster inoculation is necessary. Extra vitamin E in the diet is beneficial and can be given in the form of 10 mg tablets: one daily, crushed in the food.

Dog breeders have conflicting ideas about which is the best

time to mate a bitch in the course of her season: some try her on the ninth day, others the eleventh, and a few leave it until the fourteenth day. In fact there is a certain stage after which she will accept a dog and, in my experience, the average bitch is in peak condition for mating between the tenth and twelfth day. The signs are easily recognised. She will be unusually playful, the enlarged vulva which has hitherto been tensely swollen now softens, and the flow of blood is reduced. If there are other bitches in the house she will invite them to mount her, standing rigid with her tail turned to the side.

It is usual to take a bitch to visit the stud dog. Both animals should be on leads when they are introduced, and should be controlled until she clearly indicates that she will accept the dog, making playful overtures and turning her tail. They are then released together in an area from which they cannot escape but have room to indulge in amorous play until both are ready to mate. It is important that they are not given the opportunity to run off, because given a chance dogs instinctively seek a private place to mate and may travel some distance to find it.

Some maiden bitches become alarmed when a dog's attentions get serious but if he is experienced and, therefore, patient he will win her over without any need for human intervention. Far too many breeders hold both animals and create what is virtually a rape situation, which seems to me to be wrong. Furthermore, if a bitch will not voluntarily accept a dog this can mean that she is not at the right stage of her season to conceive, or that she has some internal stricture which would prevent mating or the normal birth of puppies. If she violently resents attempts to mate her she should be examined by a vet.

Both wild and domestic dogs 'tie' when they mate. The owner of a male dog will notice a ball-like part about half way along the penis: this is known as a 'knot' and when mating takes place this is held within the bitch by her muscular contraction. A tie lasts for up to half an hour and serves to ensure fertilisation. A dog usually turns so that the pair stand back to back during this time. However long a tie lasts there must be no interference as this could only result in pain and injury to the dogs.

It is a common practice to mate the pair again two days later, but this is really unnecessary if the dogs are, as they should be, in good condition.

After mating, the bitch should be kept quiet and calm. She can rest in the car while the owners have coffee or something stronger, and then be taken home and kept safe for the remainder of her season.

The gestation period

During the first month after mating the bitch can resume normal life, but must not be allowed to become over-tired or to indulge in jumping or rough play. When her season finishes, about two weeks after mating, she should be dosed against roundworms. These prey on young dogs but can remain in a state of suspended animation within an adult bitch if she was not successfully treated against them when a puppy. Pregnancy then triggers the worms into action in anticipation of invading the unborn puppies a few days before their birth. Not all authorities agree with me, but I have found from experience that dosing a bitch early in her pregnancy (it would be most unwise to give the necessary drug any later than two weeks) almost always prevents the puppies from being born with these worms.

A pregnant bitch and her unborn puppies will benefit from extra calcium in the diet to produce strong bones. There are various veterinary preparations on the market designed as a supplement for pregnant and lactating bitches: the chosen one should contain calcium plus vitamins A and D and must be given according to the manufacturers' instructions to avoid dangerous over-dosing.

The average gestation period in bitches is nine weeks (63 days). Live births are unlikely earlier than sixty days, and if the period is prolonged beyond sixty-five days the bitch should be examined by a vet. Days should be counted to include the mating day.

It is useful to understand what is going on inside the bitch during her pregnancy. The puppies do not lie in the uterus itself but along two branches of it known as the horns of the uterus; they lie along the belly on either side of the spine. After four weeks they begin to move down towards the floor of the abdominal cavity, and at six weeks reach their lowest point – the bitch is then said to have 'dropped' – which means that her belly is greatly enlarged; soon the puppies will be seen moving and kicking when she is lying quiet.

The bitch's diet is important. From the fourth week she should be given less bulk and more concentrated nourishment in the form of meat, milk and eggs; and from the sixth week the daily feed should be cut into three parts: milk and raw egg for breakfast, meat at midday and meat and biscuit in the evening. This does not mean that she needs more food than usual, but it should be of better quality and in smaller quantities at one time, because when she is full of puppies there is little room for the stomach to expand. It is a mistake to overfeed a pregnant bitch. At the fetal stage puppies have little effect upon her, beyond absorbing minerals, and too much bulk food may cause her to lay on fat, which can result in a difficult birth.

During the last two weeks she should be given gentle exercise walking on a lead, making sure that she is not allowed to become tired. Obviously she should not be taken on a jolting car journey.

The birth

Two or three days before their birth the puppies are generally very lively and can be seen churning about like a bagful of ferrets. The bitch's teats will have swollen and are likely to contain milk, and there may be a slight clear discharge from the vulva which is also enlarged.

Prepare a whelping bed about a week before the expected date, so that the bitch knows where it is and, if she has had puppies before, what it is for. The bed, whether it is a shallow box or a plastic dog bed, must be large enough to allow the bitch to lie full length, with space to spare. Many breeders use newspaper as bedding, but I am against this because it is not comfortable and newsprint ink is mildly poisonous if licked. I use a piece of old

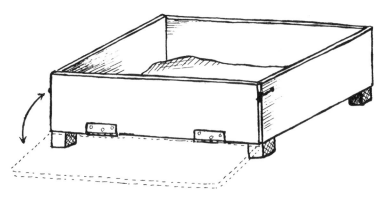

Whelping box – shallow rectangular box on short legs, with front hinged to let down as ramp

carpet as a base, covering it with a terry towel of baby's nappy size.

The bed should be in a warm but not stuffy place, and secluded from the rest of the household, particularly from children, cats and other dogs, so that the bitch is assured that this is a safe place for her litter. If she reverts to a primitive instinct and wishes to tear up the bedding to make a nest, she can be given some tissue paper to meet this need. She should be taken to the bed several times a day and encouraged to get into it so that she realises that it is for her.

Most animals (and human beings) tend to give birth in the early hours after midnight, and a bitch is no exception. However, there are usually signs some time before the event: the bitch will be restless and if she is inexperienced will be anxious, and there will be a glairy discharge from the vulva. She should be taken out to relieve herself and then returned to her prepared bed. If it is her first litter the feeling of internal pressure can mislead her into expecting a bowel movement, and she will become worried, asking to be let out again. This needs sympathetic treatment: she must be told in a reassuring voice that all is well and to lie down and be a good girl.

The owner acting as midwife needs a hand towel, a pair of blunt-end scissors and a flask of coffee for personal consumption during what may be a long night.

An experienced bitch will need little if any help – though most like to have their owner's company while they are in labour. With a first litter, however, a bitch may need help and what may be described as advice, until the birth of one or more puppies shows her what is happening: then instinct will take over.

When contractions start, she will begin to strain at intervals. Panting, blinking and twitching the ears are all signs of pain in a dog and, since labour is painful, should not cause concern. The important thing is to persuade the bitch to lie down and get on with it. The contractions will become more frequent and may be encouraged by gently stroking the bitch's flank until a dark bladder-like vessel appears as the immediate forerunner of the first puppy which is enclosed in it. At this point it is passing through the pelvis and causing the most pain until one final contraction thrusts it into the world. The majority of puppies are born within a bag and must be released. Normally, a bitch does this with her teeth, but with a first puppy it is better for the owner to do it. Either use blunt-ended scissors, with extreme care, or tear it apart with previously cleaned and scrubbed finger nails. I use the latter method, and then clear mucus from the puppy's mouth with a finger so that it can take its first gasp of air.

The puppy is still attached by its umbilical cord to the placenta (afterbirth) which has yet to be expelled. A bitch who knows what she is doing will bite through the cord by grinding it on her back molar teeth, but it is safer for the owner to sever it for the first puppy. (A friend of mine left a corgi bitch to manage on her own, with the horrifying result that she not only bit through the cord but also removed the penis of a dog puppy.)

When it is born the puppy is of course lying at the rear of the bitch; it should not be picked up but treated where it lies, because its blood supply is still connected to the placenta at this stage and raising it can mean that some of the blood may run back down the cord. The cord should be held next to the body, pinched between finger and thumb, and then severed to leave a length of about $1\frac{1}{2}$ inches still attached to the puppy. Blunt-ended scissors may be used, but I have always done this job by grinding the cord between the nails of my forefinger and thumb in much the same fashion as a bitch would use her teeth, as this method serves to seal it; a straight cut may lead to a small amount of bleeding.

If the bedding provided was thoroughly clean there is no need to put antiseptic on the cord. It will shrivel and drop off within a couple of days.

Once the puppy is free, it should be lifted up and placed near the bitch's head so that she can sniff and lick it. It is delightful to watch the dawning of comprehension in a young bitch: so this is what all that pain and struggle was about! The puppy itself instinctively searches for a milk supply and may be guided to a teat to take a first life-giving drink.

The first placenta should then appear and is normally eaten by the bitch. This is not a disgusting habit but an instinctive one which provides easily digested protein and certain hormones to activate milk production. In the case of big breeds liable to have ten or a dozen puppies, the last few placentas are removed, but a Jack Russell bitch may be allowed to eat the usual three or four.

While the first-born may have taken up to an hour to appear, succeeding puppies are likely to be born every ten minutes or quarter of an hour and, unless a bitch is clearly competent to cope with them herself, I treat each one like the first – removing it from its bag and cutting the cord.

There are two important points to watch. First, count the arrival of each placenta to ensure that none are retained; and second, call a vet within five minutes of the appearance of a bag which ruptures without a puppy being born, as this can only mean that the foetus is wrongly presented or perhaps dead, thus blocking the passage of remaining puppies.

However, such alarming happenings are rare in a sturdy breed like Jack Russell terriers. While I have never intentionally left a bitch to give birth on her own, there was one occasion when I had friends to lunch and spent about forty minutes chatting to them at the table before noticing that my bitch, due to whelp the next day, was no longer sitting beside my chair. I went in search and found her complacently lying in her bed suckling a litter of four.

A bitch may be glad of a small drink of warm milk between births, but will not need any solid food for twelve hours afterwards. Milk at intervals will sustain her meanwhile. A good first feed is made up by dissolving two baby rusks in enough warm milk to make a sloppy paste, to which may be added a raw egg. These proprietary rusks are excellent as they contain minerals and vitamins and are easily digested.

After about six hours, when the bitch has rested and the puppies are well fed and content, she may be persuaded to visit the garden to relieve herself. During this brief time a helper should replace the damp and soiled bedding with a piece of clean blanket which has been warmed. The family can now be left in peace to recover from the ordeal of giving birth and being born.

The bitch and her litter

A nursing bitch will need increasing amounts of nourishing food as her litter grows, bearing in mind that a puppy has doubled its birth weight at the age of eight days and is consuming more and more of her milk to maintain this rate of growth. As an example of the richness of bitches' milk, representative samples have been analysed from a cow and a bitch to show a fat content of 4 per cent in the former and 14·8 per cent in the latter. Clearly this output from a bitch is a drain on her resources and she must be fed accordingly.

Three days after the birth and from then onwards until the puppies are weaned, she will benefit most from meat, both raw and cooked, and milk and eggs, with the amounts of food and the number of feeds increasing to meet her appetite.

When the puppies are four days old, current fashion decrees that their tails must be docked. Many breeders of Jack Russells are giving up this practice but, until it is banned and buyers cease to expect shortened tails, undocked puppies may be difficult to sell.

The surgery should be performed by a vet who, if he is unfamiliar with the breed, should be asked to leave three-fifths of the tail, which will give the required 4 inches when the puppy is fully grown. Since the puppies must suffer this brief amount of pain anyway it is as well to have the dewclaws removed at the time. This is also a good time to clip the sharp tips of all the claws to prevent the bitch being scratched.

While all this is happening the bitch must be shut away out of earshot and occupied by a feed or a beef bone until the puppies have ceased whimpering and have settled in the safety of their bed. When she is allowed back her brood will smell of the vet and of blood and antiseptic, and it must be realised that she is liable to be upset about them being injured in her absence.

The puppies' eyes open on about the twelfth day and soon after that they will begin to crawl around and may tumble out of the bed unless the sides are high enough to prevent this. An alternative is to use a whelping box which has the front side hinged so that it can be lowered to form a ramp. This ramp should have carpet or hessian tacked to it so that a wandering puppy can creep in and out with ease. If legs are fitted to the box these must be short enough to prevent a puppy from crawling underneath and becoming lost and chilled.

At first a bitch lies down to suckle her puppies but as they grow in size and strength she may stand over them. Once they start getting about the bed must be arranged to allow them in and out to explore a fenced area.

The teeth erupt from the gums when the puppies are about three weeks old. As soon as they can be felt by inserting a finger-tip into the mouth it is time to begin weaning the puppies on to foods other than their dam's milk. Start with scraped raw meat because this is easily digested and is taken eagerly when a puppy has had a smell and taste of it. Meat should be scraped from the sinews and fat with a blunt knife (minced meat is indigestible), and made into one small ball for each puppy; the amount for a Jack Russell at this stage should be about kidney-bean size. The puppies should be fed individually outside their enclosure to ensure that they receive their allotted ration and no more. This small introductory feed is enough for the first two days; then give meat in the morning and milk in the evening. Whenever possible, warm goat's milk is best but a proprietary brand of puppy milk powder is a good alternative if it is carefully mixed according to the makers' instructions.

To begin with, lapping is difficult for a puppy, which tends to overbalance as it leans forward to drink from a dish. For this reason I use glass custard bowls, the type that have a short stem on a firm base, as a puppy can stand to drink from them – and a washed glass dish can be seen to be clean.

As soon as the puppies are taking other foods the bitch should be kept away from them for about half an hour after she has had her own meal because a number of bitches will regurgitate partially digested food for their litters. This is a reversion to the wild dog's method of weaning but is most unsuitable for domestic puppies and deprives the dam of her proper ration.

At four weeks old the puppies should have four meals a day, the amount of meat increasing to match their growth and appetite, plus two milk feeds and one of baby rusk mashed in milk. The amount to give is dictated by commonsense, allowing each puppy a satisfying feed without bloating it. As the litter takes more food the dam's milk supply must gradually dry up, and the best way to achieve this is to let her in to suckle them after they have been fed. In this way they will take less every time and she will produce less as their demands dwindle; she will have little or no milk in her teats by the time the litter is six or seven weeks old.

Lactation is very taxing on a bitch but, if she has been carefully fed with nourishing foods throughout that period, she should have remained in good condition and can be back on the usual one meal a day by the time the puppies are completely weaned. However, if she is a little thin she can be built up with paunches, rabbit, fish, and eggs. Red meat and milk should be withheld as these are liable to encourage milk production rather than put flesh on her back.

When the litter is six weeks old, rusks and milk should be replaced with puppy-grade biscuit meal moistened with meat stock or milk, and give a raw egg in one of the milk feeds.

A routine dose against roundworms should be given at this time, preferably using one of the flavoured types now on the market as a puppy will accept this voluntarily. The manufacturer's instructions must be exactly followed. Should dosing result in the appearance of worms, a repeat dose should be given four weeks later to ensure that all the parasites have been eliminated.

Most breeders sell their puppies at between eight and ten weeks old, supplying buyers with a feeding chart and notes on general care. The date of worming and the recommended time for a second dose should be added to this information.

6

Shows and Showing

Classes for Jack Russell terriers are organised at various country functions, such as exemption dog shows, hunt kennel open days, fêtes or festivals, and by branches of the breed club. These events may be seen advertised in the local and dog press, and schedules are usually available from pet shops, saddlers and the offices of agricultural merchants. Members of the club will be given advance notice in the quarterly magazine of shows to be run under club rules.

Exemption shows

An exemption dog show must be licensed by the Kennel Club but is exempt from their basic rule that all dogs must be pedigree and registered. Four pedigree classes are allowed and these are mainly of use to breeders as a means of introducing young dogs to the show world without subjecting them to the long hours and general noise and bustle of a big event.

The remaining classes are for fun rather than prestige, allowing family pets of any breed or crossbreed to compete. Because they are not recognised by the Kennel Club, Jack Russell terriers must be entered in this second category, either in mixed classes or in a class for them alone.

This type of show offers a good introduction to showing for a Jack Russell and its owner. The only disadvantage can be that the appointed judge may not be conversant with the breed standard if his or her experience has been only with KC breeds.

Even so, there is much to be learned from taking part in any kind of dog show: there is more to it than merely standing about in the ring holding a dog on a lead.

Any animal, whether a horse, a pig or a Jack Russell terrier, entered for exhibition must be put before the judge looking its best if it is to have a chance of success. In my opinion it is an insult to expect a judge to take a serious interest in a grubby, ungroomed dog. On the other hand, the majority of judges are kind and helpful to an obviously bewildered novice owner with no idea of ring procedure.

Most small shows are held out of doors in the summer and early autumn, but the venue for some winter events may be a village hall or similar building. In general, outdoor events with grassed rings are best suited to Jack Russells, which may not move well on a polished floor.

Preparation and ring-craft

The first essential in a dog that is to show itself properly is lead training. It must walk sensibly on its owner's left side, neither pulling forward nor back, nor leaping about: it is impossible to judge the conformation and movement of a terrier that is running askew, hauling on its lead. At the same time, it must look alert and happy, and not dejected by too much discipline. The objective is to produce an animal with what is known in the horse world as 'presence' – an attitude of 'Here I am, look at me ... the greatest!' A judge is only human and is likely to be attracted to a self-confident but well-mannered dog.

Cleanliness is the next point. A dog kept indoors and given a clean bed will need little grooming before a show, unless it is moulting its coat at the time; as a rule, all that is needed is a light brushing to remove loose hairs and dust. But if the dog has been out in muddy weather or has been digging in a rabbit burrow, it may have to be given a dressing of grooming powder, well rubbed into the coat and then thoroughly brushed out. Smooth-coated dogs can be given a final gloss by wiping over with a chamois leather or piece of silky material.

The Reverend John Russell, founder of the breed which bears his name. The type he favoured has largely been replaced by a somewhat smaller, more compact dog, but the name is a fitting tribute to his work in establishing the Jack Russell

A trio of cheerful workers ready for anything

The dog on the right has correct drop ears. Its companion has pricked ears, a common fault as all wild dogs have pricked ears. In short-haired terriers, a folded ear is preferable because it is less likely to get clogged with earth underground (*Panther Photographic International*)

While those who exhibit dogs under KC rules must use special show leads with collars attached, Jack Russell terriers are shown in ordinary leather collars and leather or light chain leads. The leather should be plain, not coloured.

The organisers of small shows take entries 'on the field': that is, on the show day during the hour or so before judging begins. Each competitor is given a ring number and it is worth remembering to bring a safety-pin so that the number can be pinned to a lapel or other suitable part of the clothing.

When judging starts, a steward will call out the numbers of those entered in the first class and allow a few minutes for the exhibitors to congregate in the ring, but there is no redress for anyone who wanders off to watch some other event or visit the beer tent. Dogs and their handlers then walk anti-clockwise round the ring, each dog walking on the left to be in view of the judge, who stands in the centre with a steward.

This initial walk round gives the judge a look at the class as a whole, with an opportunity to pick out likely dogs from the no-hopers, and so it is important for a dog to go well at this stage. Jack Russells, particularly bitches, are inclined to waddle if they are walked at too slow a pace and must be taken along at a near-trot to produce the best action. This is sometimes difficult in a mixed-breed class which perhaps includes a peke and an alsatian, one going too slowly and the other too fast. It is permissible to bypass the peke on the outside (not blocking it from the judge's view) and to allow the alsatian to go ahead to show its paces.

An exhibitor who has taken the trouble to do some training at home will know that the dog is moving well and therefore should keep an eye not on it but on the judge and steward, one of whom will call a halt to the walk round and require the dogs to be taken to form a line at one side of the ring.

Then, usually beginning on the right, each entry in turn is called in to be examined by the judge. He or she will go over it from front to back – looking at the teeth, eyes and expression and feeling its body structure. The handler is now asked to take it 'up and back', which means going away from the judge in a straight line and back again, so that the action can be seen from the back and the front. The handler then returns to the line.

Bad behaviour often creeps in at this juncture if there is a large entry in the class. Waiting while others are judged may be boring but must not tempt a handler to light a cigarette or chat with other exhibitors or onlookers. A dog and its handler may relax to some extent, but it must be borne in mind that judging a class is a matter of comparison and a judge may glance back to the line while examining one dog to see how it compares with another, and if the second animal happens to be asleep or sitting down scratching itself it may be forgotten.

Ring manners are vital. Exhibitors should remember that judges at small shows almost always receive no fee and some even waive their travelling expenses; they have a right to expect politeness. In essence, this involves watching the judge's every move and responding promptly and cheerfully to orders, and keeping a dog on its toes. Manners towards fellow exhibitors are equally important: it is not unknown for one person to place a dog in front of another, or to use a squeaky toy to gain a dog's attention. Such behaviour is inadmissible but there are 'tricks of the trade' which can legitimately make a dog alert during a tedious pause in the proceedings. A plastic bag containing a few morsels of cold fried liver works wonders – a dog trained to expect titbits of this delicacy will look keen, tail wagging, and put on a better show than its neighbour. Here again, it would be most unfair to allow that neighbour a whiff of such a prize, which might encourage it to behave badly.

When all the dogs have been examined a select few are called forward so that the judge can make a final decision. The steward will thank the rest, who should retire with good grace. Those remaining should stand in line, offering a side view to the judge, who will look at each in turn. Sometimes judging is simplified by the fact that there are four outstanding animals with the certainty of a prize between first and reserve (fourth), and the decision is between best and second best, and so on. But a large class may force a judge to bring forward six or eight dogs in order to make a final choice.

In this make-or-break situation an exhibitor must keep calm

and listen to instructions. The judge is likely to go over the dog again from head to tail, and then ask for it to be taken up and back in a triangle. A flustered handler may then set off to the left and so cross the top of the triangle with the dog hidden from view by human legs, instead of going right, left, and left again to arrive back in front of the watching judge, the dog then having been seen from the rear, the side, and the front.

If its action is passed as satisfactory, a dog is now assessed for conformation and temperament, and this is where a good stance and a wagging tail pay dividends. The handler has done his or her best and it is up to the judge to choose.

There are those who insist that, win or lose, an exhibitor should remain poker-faced. Certainly a bad loser either appears ridiculous or an embarrassment to other people, but there is no harm in being delighted at winning any one of the rosettes and sharing this triumph with the dog by patting and praising it. This behaviour, in moderation, will please onlookers, whereas a person who accepts a prize (especially a trophy) with a blank expression may be thought arrogant.

Breed shows

Regional branches of the Jack Russell Club of Great Britain organise shows within their area. Sometimes these are held in conjunction with another event, such as a horse show or a hunt hound show, and they often include classes for other kinds of dog: for example, for lurchers, working border and lakeland terriers and 'family dogs' – a euphemism for any breed, crossbreed or mongrel. These shows are not under licence from the Kennel Club, but the Jack Russell classes are judged according to the breed standard.

The owner of a Jack Russell, seriously interested in the breed, may use an exemption show as a schooling ground, but a breed show is far more rewarding because here the dog is given expert assessment and a prize really means something; and there is the added pleasure of meeting other enthusiasts and making friends.

Schedules are subject to permutation but generally the classes are grouped under the two height standards and further divided by classes for dogs and for bitches, smooth and rough or broken-coated. A champion and reserve champion are selected from the first-prize winners as a whole.

Further classes are likely to include one for veteran dogs, over eight years old; one for child handlers; a brace class; and perhaps a progeny class for two or three generations. In addition there may be a class for Parson Jack Russell terriers to be won by a dog or bitch which most resembles the parson's ideal: that is, being approximately 14 inches high and 14 pounds in weight, with a coat that is a trifle wiry.

Organising a small show

Establishing even a small dog show involves a good deal of work. In country districts the best plan is to join up with some other show, such as a flower show or gymkhana, because this will simplify the organisation, providing a ready-made venue and attracting more people to pay at the gate – those who would not cross a road to see a dog show may well buy a ticket for the other event in a joint venture and find themselves equally interested in the dogs when they get there.

The first step is to attend a meeting of the existing show committee and put forward the proposition that an event for dogs would be an added attraction. If this is agreed the next stage is to form a sub-committee to run the dog show.

Over the years I have been inveigled into acting as secretary and show manager for various dog shows, from a large open show to a small village event, and experience has taught me that an average committee consists of a minority of doers and a majority of talkers. I now organise an annual show in conjunction with a horse show and find that an unorthodox form of procedure works better. Two friends and I meet at home to decide on the schedule and who will do what. Then each takes on certain tasks which normally would be the job of a secretary: these include obtaining a KC licence (as it is an exemption show), obtaining ring numbers and rosettes, begging for trophies and prizes in kind, advertising and printing schedules, and persuading a good judge that it would be fun to have a day out with us in return for a bottle of Scotch.

When all this has been achieved we return to the main committee with the preliminary work done and ask for sturdier members to arrange one or perhaps two rings to our specification and bench seats for exhibitors and spectators. In this kind of set-up there is no need for a treasurer to the sub-committee as all the funds accumulate to the show as a whole and the horse-show treasurer provides money required in the initial stages.

On the day itself more helpers are needed and then we draw on people who are bored by the organisational side of the show but quite prepared to act as stewards or undertake other odd jobs. This comparatively easy way to arrange a show may not appeal to those who like to 'go by the book', but it works well – provided that all those who promised help at the show itself are true to their word.

Ring sizes are sometimes a source of argument. The minimum should be about 20 feet (7 metres) by 30 feet (10 metres), depending on the expected number of entries. Some show organisers do not mark out a ring, leaving it to spectators to form a rough circle, but this can be unsatisfactory because there is nothing to prevent people from wandering across while judging is in progress. A few posts supporting a single line of rope or coloured string will mark the ring as out of bounds to all but the competitors, judge and steward.

The dog-show officials need a table and a few chairs at the ring-side. Trophies and rosettes are displayed on this table, which is also used for taking entry money and recording exhibitors' numbers and classes entered. The cash box will need a float of money for change purposes.

Recording entries may be done in several ways but I find the simplest is to have a reporter's notepad and head each blank page with the various classes from one onwards. Each exhibitor's number is then marked on the appropriate pages for the classes in which they have entered. As judging proceeds the pages are torn out and given to the judge's steward who calls out the numbers, marks the winning dogs' numbers, and returns it to the table. When the time comes to judge 'best' and 'reserve best' in show and apportion the trophies offered for specific wins (such as best veteran or best child handler), the sheaf of pages is handed back to the steward so that the judge can easily identify the unbeaten dogs.

Among the various classes the one for child handlers is a special case. There should be the usual rosettes for the first four places and consolation prizes for all the rest, so that no child leaves the ring empty-handed. I have a vivid memory of being asked to judge a fancy-dress class at a gymkhana. There were four rosettes and nineteen hopeful entrants sitting on ponies and dressed as Robin Hood, Bo-Peep and whoever; my job was to choose and then make a run for it before a lynch mob of disappointed mothers caught up with me. Small bags of sweets or candy for the losers defuse this situation.

Parking facilities need consideration. At an outdoor show exhibitors prefer to park their cars near the ring so that dogs can be kept in them when not actively engaged in the show. This needs a helper who can combine authority with diplomacy to prevent chaos being caused by the inevitable few people intent on parking at right angles to everybody else, blocking both entrance and exit.

When the money taken in entry fees has been totalled at the end of the day it is important to remember to extract various expenses (the judge's gift, lunch and travelling, and special prizes for the children's class) before handing the profit to the treasurer. Everything relating to cash and winning exhibitors must be recorded at the time because, for instance, the name and address of the winner of a perpetual trophy may be forgotten next year and also the local press will want to know the winners of each class.

Terrier racing

Jack Russell terrier racing is often organised as an added attraction in country events and is solely for the amusement of the dogs, their owners and spectators who enjoy watching game little dogs in hot pursuit of a stuffed rabbit skin over a distance of a hundred yards or more.

A handyman can easily make sets of starting traps which will open simultaneously at the pull of a lever. There are various methods employed to drag the dummy rabbit: probably the best way is to attach it to a long cord leading to a rear wheel (from which the tyre has been removed) of a jacked-up vehicle. The driver can watch the dogs and rev the engine so that the dummy is still ahead when they cross the finishing line. Bicycles have been rigged up in a similar fashion but require a lot of energy on the part of the pedaller.

The drawback to racing Jack Russells is that they are liable to become quarrelsome when excited which can result in a fight at the finish unless they are all being well supervised there.

7

Terriers in Sport

Jack Russell terriers will go to ground whenever they are given the opportunity to dig out a quarry, whether it be a rat, a rabbit or a fox. Until otter hunting and badger digging were made illegal they were also employed against these animals. Conservationists were relieved when the hunting of otters was banned because these beautiful and relatively harmless creatures were on the brink of extinction in Britain. Such otter hunts as remain now hunt mink: fierce little predators which really are harmful to poultry and wildlife. A terrier that will tackle a mink has to be tough indeed, but most Jack Russells will do it.

The mink is not indigenous to Britain and the feral population all descend from animals that have escaped from fur farms. It is a member of the varied family *Mustelidae* which includes badgers, otters, stoats, weasels, pine-martens, polecats and the domesticated ferret, and combines the aquatic habits of the otter with the temperament of a stoat.

I have seen mink in the wild on two occasions, mistaking one of them at first sight for a black cat slinking along a ditch until I had taken a closer look and then chosen the better part of valour with undignified haste. Some years ago, when I had charge of a small zoo, a kindly couple arrived carrying a box emitting scrabbling noises and told me that they had found an unconscious baby otter on the river bank and this was it, now revived. Fortunately the box was placed in a spare cage before the lid was opened, because out leaped a very angry young mink. On the principle that almost all young animals become tame in

84

captivity, I kept this one for several months while it thrived and grew, but it retained an almost maniacal desire to attack every living thing within its view, tearing at the wire mesh of the cage with its teeth, and eventually I decided that the only humane solution was to shoot this very wild creature which could not be released.

Otter hounds hunt mink in much the same way as they hunted otters: following a scent left by the animal's nocturnal wanderings until the burrow in the bank of a stream where it lies up is traced. Terriers are then put in and spades used to dislodge the mink, which is then hunted by the hounds and their followers who enjoy good sport of an energetic and rather wetting kind. The drawback, from the conservation point of view, is that the remaining otters share the same habitat as mink and hunting inevitably disturbs them; they cannot even know that they are no longer the quarry.

Badgers, too, made ferocious protagonists, with an ability to lock their jaws after taking hold of an adversary, which meant that terriers used for badger-digging were often killed. Badger-digging was a repulsive pastime which cannot be dignified by the title of sport, because it involved great cruelty and no chance of escape for the victim unless the 'sett' or burrow was an old one with extensive tunnels and galleries. Several terriers were used to worry the badger underground until it could be reached by digging with spades.

The Athenian Xenophon, writing more than 300 years before the Christian era, laid down a code of conduct for sportsmen which included a fair run for the hunted animal. It is to our shame that badger-digging was popular enough in the English Westcountry to warrant the formation of the Devon and Somerset Badger Club in 1894 for the avowed purpose of promoting an interest in the 'sport'. Its other interest was in breeding game working terriers, and after World War I the name of the club was altered to the Parson Jack Russell Terrier Club, using as a logo a circle containing the figures 14 : 14 on either side of a dividing line – to represent the ideal height and weight of the terrier type preferred by Jack Russell himself.

This club petered out in the course of time and has recently been replaced by the modern Jack Russell Terrier Club of Great Britain, with updated standards.

Foxhunting

Most hunts keep their own terriers, which are in the charge of a terrier man who is aiso responsible for earth-stopping. He may be a hunt servant or a supporter who does the job for love of the sport.

In truth, many of those who enjoy foxhunting would like to see the animal left in peace if it reaches the sanctuary of its earth, preferring to see it killed in the open or not at all. The problem is that a pack must kill as many foxes as it can to make up for the nuisance caused in the countryside by hounds and their mounted followers – disturbing lambing ewes and so on. So once a fox has gone to ground, digging-out is the only alternative, and this is where the terriers come on the scene. The master blows a call on his horn to bring them and, when they arrive, takes the hounds back some distance to await events. With luck the fox may be induced to bolt and given the hounds another run and a clean kill if the quarry fails to elude them, but usually the animal has to be dug out with spades.

Diggers are guided by a terrier which is baying the fox underground, after entering the earth and tracking its enemy by scent in pitch darkness. A good terrier barks continuously as it drives the fox until the animal is cornered, when the note changes to a frenzy and informs the people above that here is the place to dig. The terrier must not attack but keep the fox at bay, lying about two feet away; if it is fighting it will be silent and, therefore, lost to the diggers – and it may receive crippling injuries into the bargain. When the diggers come down to the dog it is removed and the fox is promptly shot with a humane-killer pistol.

That, in brief, is what happens with an experienced terrier. A young dog must learn its work by degrees: first held on a lead, watching older dogs and getting used to hounds, horses and the general excitement of the day. It should not be entered to a fox until it is adult in size and strength, which means being not less than about eighteen months old. After a few such occasions when the dog should be showing a keen interest in the proceedings, it may be allowed to sniff a shot fox to learn that this is the quarry.

The next stage involves meeting a live fox head on, and this can be done when diggers reach a baying terrier and remove it, replacing it with the young one. It is important to control the dog to prevent it from rushing in and getting badly bitten by the fox, and yet achieve a confrontation that will be remembered. A novice terrier whose first experience has been a battle with a bayed fox may react in one of two ways, both bad – either losing its nerve or becoming an inveterate fighter underground.

When a terrier is released into an earth to work for the first time, its collar must be removed to avoid the chance of snagging, and it must be handled calmly: not cheered on but just quietly encouraged, because terriers are excitable enough as it is and one that charges into an earth like a bull at a gate is unlikely to work intelligently.

A Master of Foxhounds interested in the Jack Russell breed may be prepared to give a privately owned dog a working certificate after it has proved itself an efficient worker in the course of a hunt, and this will be noted when the dog is registered in the JRT Club's advanced register by the Breed Records Officer. The same type of certificate may be signed by the Master of a pack of otter (mink) hounds.

Terriers and ferrets

Working two different kinds of animal together is always fascinating. A classic example is an English pointer working with a peregrine falcon to hunt grouse, but on a more mundane level rabbiting with terriers and ferrets is an entertaining sport – though it is not an efficient way of clearing a warren.

If they have been properly introduced, and the dogs are obedient, terriers and ferrets get on with each other well on the basis of mutual respect, but the first few meetings must be supervised. At first sight a dog may be forgiven for thinking that a ferret is some form of rat and react accordingly, the ferret will respond by attacking the dog with all the natural courage that these little animals possess. The result is likely to be a dead ferret and a badly bitten terrier.

When I introduce some new animal to my dogs I use the words, 'No, pet', in a firm voice. Each dog is then allowed to sniff the creature while I repeat the command. In the case of a ferret, it should be held in one hand and the dog controlled by its collar with the other. The distinctive smell of a ferret is soon learned by an intelligent dog.

The correct way to handle a ferret is to hold it round the neck between forefinger and thumb, with the remaining three fingers round the chest behind its front legs, leaving the hindquarters dangling. This is comfortable for the animal if it is handled gently and not gripped, and a young ferret soon becomes as tame as a kitten provided that it is always treated kindly and not subjected to sudden moves which may alarm it. A bite from a ferret is not easily forgotten, particularly since it hangs on with teeth that will reach the bone: the bitten person must somehow remain calm and stoical, not pulling away but using soothing words in place of the expletives that will come to mind, until the animal lets go. If it persists, it can be forced to open its jaws by giving one of its front feet a severe pinch. A ferret that bites more than once for no good reason should be disposed of and replaced by a younger, well-handled animal.

Male and female ferrets are known as 'dogs' and 'bitches', or in England as 'hobs' and 'jills'. There are two types: the polecat or fitch-ferret, which descends from the wild polecat of the British Isles, a brownish animal with cream markings; and the albino, which has pink eyes and yellowy-cream fur. In my experience, both sexes of both types are equally good for hunting. The drawback to a jill, most owners believe, is that she should be allowed to breed or she may pine and die soon after her second season, which occurs in the spring.

Anyone who proposes to keep ferrets should bear in mind that killing is their sole aim in life. As an example, on one occasion I had just bought fifty point-of-lay pullets at some considerable expense and a few hours later found that twenty of them had been systematically destroyed by my excited jill, aided and abetted by her family of kits, which had escaped from their casually latched hutch and discovered the fowls' house.

When hunting rabbits or rats a dog must learn to sit and stay sitting until told to do something else, because quiet waiting is part and parcel of successful ferreting, which involves bolting the quarry from its burrow.

Rabbit warrens are usually located in banks, among tree roots in a coppice or in natural or man-made hummocks of ground; they may be in any well-drained spot where the burrows are unlikely to be flooded. An occupied warren can be recognised by freshly dug earth and signs of rabbit droppings. A single burrow partially obscured by a covering of dried grass and moss should be left alone as it is almost certainly a doe's nest burrow. Even leaving aside humanitarian aspects, putting in a ferret will result in a boring wait while it feasts on the helpless young and then sleeps off the banquet.

A true warren consists of several burrows, which can be readily seen, and an emergency bolt-hole, often hidden by grass tussocks or brambles, some distance from the main entrances. The burrows should be approached quietly from up-wind and one or two ferrets put in at separate holes, while obedient dogs are placed at strategic points and those less reliable held on slip-leads. Rabbits will appear quite soon, some bolting like bullets to be pursued by the loose terriers on the command 'Seek!'; others may creep from one entrance to another or lurk in an opening, clearly undecided whether to bolt or go back down the burrow. These should be left alone, as good ferrets will bolt them clear in the end to become prey for the terriers held in reserve.

This kind of rabbiting complies with Xenophon's principles, because enthusiastic terriers, running in all directions, will miss as many rabbits as they catch, but it is fun for all concerned – except for the rabbits. As for the carcasses of the killed rabbits, these are likely to be mangled to a greater or lesser extent, perhaps leaving only the rear end, including the meaty hindlegs, suitable for the table, but the remainder can be cooked for the dogs or taken to feed raw to ferrets.

Rats are a constant nuisance in barns and stables, where they eat or pollute valuable feeding-stuffs and are a source of disease. The problem with rats from the dog owner's point of view is that up to 50 per cent of a given population can be carriers of leptospiral jaundice, which will infect an uninoculated dog and probably prove fatal. Terriers used for ratting must be inoculated and given necessary booster injections at intervals in order to be safe.

Ferreting for rats is carried out in much the same way as rabbiting in warrens. The proceedings must be quiet and the dogs controlled until the rats bolt. A good terrier will seize a rat by the back of the neck and shake it to death within seconds, but a young one must learn the art and, meanwhile, it is important to see that it is not unnerved by an unpleasant experience. A puppy should be at least eight months old and reasonably obedient before it is allowed to take part in a rat hunt. All dogs which have been involved in ratting should be inspected for possible bites, which should be swabbed with a solution of antiseptic to guard against infection.

Jack Russell terriers are not aggressive by nature, but if one is provoked it will go into battle with flags flying and this is worth remembering when an excited group is in the midst of killing bolting rats or digging in a burrow. If an individual loses its temper the result is liable to be an all-out scrap, which means that any signs of tension must be nipped in the bud by removing the angry dog and shutting it away. On one occasion two of my bitches went on a ratting expedition in a barn, without my knowledge until one reappeared covered in earth and dust. When I asked, 'Where's Minny?', she cringed and retired under a chair. I found the missing bitch lying unconscious in the barn, flecked with blood, and with her tongue a dark blue colour which indicated heart failure. Evidently they had fought over who should dig in a particular burrow. The vet gave Minny injections and a fifty-fifty chance of survival, but such is the toughness of the Jack Russell breed that she rallied and lived on into old age.

The ridiculous part of the story is that the two were inseparable friends until this quarrel triggered a fight almost to the death; it serves as a reminder that when terriers embark on fighting there is no knowing where it will end.

Rabbiting with terriers

Since myxomatosis, the rabbit population in England and Wales has so declined that they have become rare in some parts of the country. However, in places plenty of rabbits still thrive, plaguing farmers and providing sport for those who have several dogs to make up a bobbery pack to hunt rabbits after the fashion of beagling.

At one time I used to take out a dalmatian, a beagle and several Jack Russell terriers on rabbit hunts and found it an enjoyable, often hilarious, sport, with the added interest of watching different dogs working together for a common purpose. I have seen a rabbit retire into a patch of undergrowth, shown its line to the dogs and then stood back to watch what appeared to be extra-sensory perception lead each dog to take up a position which meant that the pack would effectively surround the quarry, while one individual went in to drive it out.

My role was to find likely places where a rabbit might be hiding and shout a *view holloa* if it emerged unseen by the dogs. When it went off through long grass the pack would leap like dolphins trying to get a glimpse of it, looking at me to point the way, knowing that I was taller and possibly omniscient.

All this is great fun, but the dogs must be obedient so that they will respond promptly to a call or whistle. An unruly pack may frighten sheep, cause a traffic accident, or run headlong over a cliff's edge.

Finally, a point which may seem obvious: permission to go rabbiting on a farmer's land must be obtained, because, although rabbits are vermin, no one is going to welcome a bobbery hunt trespassing amongst crops and livestock. If you wish to be allowed to come on this owner's land again, you need to show that you understand the need to keep dogs tightly under control, shut gates and so on.

Shooting with terriers

Shooting over terriers needs the greatest care and self-control; it is quite different from sport with trained gundogs. It is the nature of a terrier to chase, usually giving tongue at the top of its voice, which means that it can all too easily be shot by someone aiming at a rabbit without due thought about where its pursuer might be.

The best way is to put a dog, or dogs, into thick undergrowth, such as a bramble patch, and shoot only at the rabbits that bolt clear while the dogs are still in the covert. This will ensure against accidents provided that your guests fully understand the arrangement.

While a working terrier must be obedient, there is no sense in attempting to train a Jack Russell as if it were a spaniel. A gundog easily learns not to chase but to drop to shot (lie down at the sound of a shot and remain there until commanded to seek and retrieve); it will do this because, basically, it is not a killer. A terrier's one aim, however, is to hunt and destroy, and if its owner tries to block this instinct too much the result will be a cowed dog which has lost its *raison d'être* and become disheartened.

A powerful jaw and a skull that allows plenty of room for brains are features of the Jack Russell (*Panther Photographic International*)

Busy Lizzie looks after the five pups of her daughter Lazy Daisy

Englebert with his glittering prizes. This dog, sire of many prize-winning puppies, was an example of the breed's longevity. On several occasions he won both a veteran class and championship on the same day

Jack Russells are adaptable dogs – equally content as companions or workers in the hunting field. They may prove ideal for a new scheme to provide guide dogs for the deaf, which needs dogs capable of learning to indicate the source of a sound such as a doorbell, alarm or telephone (*Panther Photographic International*)

8
Problem Dogs

It is often said that there are no bad dogs, only bad owners. This is an absurd theory, inferring that there is a stereotype dog with a standard temperament and amount of intelligence, capable of being moulded by correct training or ruined by mismanagement. In truth, dogs are like people: most are nice and reasonably intelligent; some are very clever; others are stupid or even mentally deficient; and a few are criminals because of their inheritance or environment.

The Jack Russell terrier and the working sheepdog have an advantage in common: the ancestors of both breeds were chosen for their intelligence, ability and hardiness, and not bred, or inbred, for show points. However, breeding for courage and tenacity in working terriers has resulted in the production of some wilful individuals, and these can become 'problem dogs' unless they are handled with care and understanding. If such a dog has been mismanaged from puppyhood it is often difficult and sometimes impossible to cure its bad habits.

Two experiences of my own illustrate the difficulties. One resulted in success and the other in dismal failure. In the first instance I was asked by two elderly ladies if I could 'do something' about their terrier. Jack the terrier was in complete charge of their household and had done what he liked since he was a puppy, so that any form of obedience was outside his experience. The net result was that his owners could not feel affection for an animal that was nothing more than a nuisance, while he was contemptuous of them. This was not a happy situation for all concerned; perhaps most of all for the dog, since dogs, like children, thrive on love and security.

Teaching Jack the rudiments of obedience seemed to be a tall order. However, I put him on a lead and we departed together to the privacy of an orchard, where I loosed him, waited until he had trotted away some distance, and then called his name in a peremptory voice. Nothing happened, not even a flick of his ears. I picked up a partially rotten fallen apple, called sharply and at the same instant shied the apple at his retreating rear end. When it hit him fair and square on the behind he uttered a yelp from shock and turned towards me. I responded with cries of sympathy and he came to me to be petted and stroked and told what a ghastly thing it was to be struck by a meteorite.

Perhaps due to a misspent youth playing darts in village pubs, I can throw quite accurately and so it was possible to repeat this episode several times – always calling and sending the missile when I was certain that Jack could not associate it with me. This was a minor and primitive form of brain-washing, but it worked. Soon, and from the two ladies' point of view miraculously, the little dog was instantly obedient to my call.

A major problem remained: I had to teach Jack's owners to give up tones of cajolery and *command* obedience instead, always meeting a response with praise and affection. I kept my magic initial training method to myself, airily dismissing questions by saying that I was used to dogs. In fact, I had tried this method for lack of any other ideas about how to deal with a spoilt two-year-old dog who was set in his ways. Puppies must be taught by constant kindness to become companionable adult dogs, and I would never suggest to anyone that throwing things at them was a good idea.

That story had a happy ending, but the next did not. I called on my vet to pick up medicine for a pony and saw a rough-haired Jack Russell tied up in a corner and naturally asked about him. The vet, a lady, said casually, 'He's been brought in to be put down. I'll do him in a minute.' This was a friendly, apparently healthy dog of about three years old, understandably looking worried after having been left by his owners in a strange place smelling of disinfectant. My heart went out to him and my commonsense flew out of the window. I said, 'I'll take him'. 'I thought you might,' said the vet with a bland smile. I knew then that she had postponed his final injection, knowing that I was due in her surgery.

The dog, whose name was Raf (his former master was in the RAF) gladly came with me, sitting on my knee while I drove him home, and soon made friends with my other dogs and settled down as if he had lived with me all his life. The only outward sign of his traumatic experience was in his anxiety to be with me wherever I went.

I kept him under close control for the first week to ensure that he would not wander, and then relaxed my vigilance until he appeared at the kitchen door carrying a mangled chicken. I took it from him, gave him a hard smack and a scolding, and then put him on a lead to go over to the fowls' enclosure for a once-for-all lesson about not killing poultry. He had burrowed under the wire netting to create havoc amongst the unfortunate birds, some of which were dead and others injured.

Raf cringed, wagging apologies and looking at me with devoted brown eyes. I took him to each dead bird in turn, shook him by the scruff and made dreadful noises of fury. We then returned to the house with him still in disgrace, where he remained shut up for an hour and was then forgiven. A long line was attached to his collar and we went back to look at the fowls; I was ready to command 'No!' and give the line a severe jerk if he showed the slightest aggression towards them. Nothing happened, and I told him that he was a good dog and assumed that one lesson had been enough.

Next morning he brought a dead mandarin duck into the house, one of several ornamental waterfowl which I kept. I smacked him, cursed him, and followed the same routine. He was abject in his apologies. In the course of trial and error over a period of two months I found that he was intelligent enough to know that a long line prohibited poultry-killing, but nothing would prevent him from attacking any feathered creature once he was loose – even if I was present to yell abuse. Something seemed to click in his brain and away he went, hell-bent on slaughter.

Knowing that a dog that kills birds has no place in the country (not to mention the fact that I was suffering financial loss), I tried every known means of curing Raf of his maniacal desire to kill chickens, ducks and even geese – finally resorting to the somewhat cruel practice of attaching a dead fowl to his collar, so that he was forced to drag the corpse about with him for a whole day.

Inevitably, the time came when he and I went to visit the vet and I came home alone, very sad after having held and comforted him while he received an injection that gave him painless and instant oblivion. This was a drastic solution but the alternatives were worse: he could have been kept shut in or on a lead for the rest of his life, or been given away to yet another home where he might have got into more trouble. Certainly he had an uncontrollable streak in his otherwise charming character.

These two stories serve as examples of different types of problem dogs. The first was a terrier which had been allowed to get out of hand but was a sensible animal and therefore was still trainable at the age of two; the second had probably been mismanaged since puppyhood, which might have aggravated the problems where fowls were concerned, but he was also the victim of a form of inborn lunacy which no amount of training, however severe, could have cured.

Anyone who has bred litters of puppies will know that as soon as the little creatures are able to see and hear they become responsive to human beings: wagging their tails and wriggling with pleasure when a fuss is made of them. A puppy that does not behave in this way is a very suspect animal indeed. But, sadly, 'there is many a slip between cup and lip' and it is all too easy to ruin a promising dog with too much or too little discipline during its formative months.

An average intelligent puppy which is brought up to expect loving kindness in return for obedience to certain rules of behaviour will respond with an innate desire to please its owner, provided that it knows what is expected of it by being taught the meaning of a set of words of command. Conversely, if varied commands are given for one required action – 'Sit', 'Lie down', 'Go away', 'Get off!' – then the result will be bewilderment and, eventually, sullen disobedience because there is a lack of mutual understanding. Such a puppy is well on the way to becoming a problem dog.

Since the Jack Russell is a highly intelligent and courageous breed with a history of fighting and badger-baiting behind it, some badly brought-up individuals can be wilful and on a hair-trigger where fighting and biting are concerned.

Fighting

A Jack Russell terrier seldom initiates a fight outside its own territory if it has been sensibly handled since puppyhood. But an owner who is over-anxious to stop it becoming involved in a battle often merely succeeds in starting one between two dogs who would have met, had a brief chat, and then gone their separate ways if left alone.

One of the best ways to make a dog quarrelsome is to pull it away from others when it is on a lead or, worse still, pick it up when another appears. There is a transfer of anxiety, which triggers an aggressive guarding instinct in the dog; it begins to

Prelude to a fight

hurl abuse and to struggle to get at the supposed enemy. A few sessions like this will make a reckless fighter out of a normally quite friendly terrier, and curing this kind of aggression is often difficult.

Left to themselves dogs have a code of conduct when they meet. This can be seen in a city park where numerous dogs are being exercised off the lead: they meet, sniff each other's scent glands, and then either play or trot away. A fight is very rare. Of course, there are criminal dogs and equally criminal owners. I met one lady owner of a Great Dane who told me, with a suggestion of pride, that this animal 'would kill small dogs ... such a nuisance!' Fortunately such dogs and people are in a minority.

When two owners meet, each with a dog on a lead, the dogs should be given an opportunity to sniff noses without any sense of tension, while the humans in the party talk to one another. If either dog is unfriendly both animals should be scolded but not pulled away; the reason for a dual scolding is that the innocent one may otherwise think that this is a signal to attack, whereas if both dogs are berated they maintain an equal status. This may seem a complicated piece of psychology but it is in line with the working of a dog's mind, which is sometimes irrational from a human standpoint.

As with any rule, there are exceptions to this one. For example, I would be very cautious about allowing a Jack Russell to meet a strange alsatian or Staffordshire bull terrier, because not only are there some bad strains within these breeds (and some others with police-dog or fighting ancestory) but a few owners positively encourage aggressiveness in them. (The culprits are usually men, apparently using hoodlum dogs as symbols of their masculinity.) Some meeker dogs finding themselves up against a bully will turn and run and thus survive, but the courage of a Jack Russell can lead it into a disastrous conflict.

Owners who keep more than one Jack Russell of the same sex may come up against jealousy at home, resulting in occasional fights. This is tiresome and difficult to cure once established, and so every effort should be made to prevent any cause for jealousy.

Even if the dogs are owned by two different members of a household, each should receive the same amount of attention and abide by the same rules – for example, one should not be a lapdog while the other must lie on the hearthrug. It is really a matter of common sense and imagination to stop resentment building up to boil over into a fight.

Stopping a fight

A dog fight is an unnerving business which often leads frightened owners to do the wrong thing, with the result that they themselves are bitten while the battle continues unabated. The first essential is to try to remain calm and to act decisively: nothing will be achieved by hitting the contestants or shouting at them, because in the frenzy of a fight a dog will think that a blow came from its adversary and shouts may be taken for encouragement.

The best method of parting fighters depends on how well matched they are and whether there is more than one person present. If two people can work in unison to stop a fight between

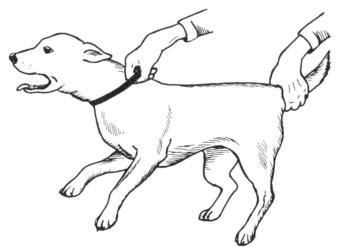

Handling a fighting terrier – fingers of one hand through the collar while the other holds the dog's tail close to the root

a pair of Jack Russells they must bear in mind that this breed locks-on with its jaws and so pulling them apart may make worse wounds. Each person should grip a dog by the tail close to the base and use the other hand to put a tourniquet twist on the collar, which will make the dogs gasp for breath and so release their holds.

When terriers are locked in combat and neither is wearing a collar, another form of partial suffocation can be effective: instead of pulling the animals apart, both are thrust against each other so that their noses are blocked and again they must gasp for breath. Fine judgement is needed in order to snatch them back at that precise second.

Pepper and buckets of water are often recommended as means of stopping a fight, but a pepper-pot is seldom to hand and I have never found that dowsing with water has the slightest effect. However, on an occasion when a fight started in my stable yard and I was single-handed, dumping both dogs into a water butt had the desired effect because they were out of their depth and forced to swim to avoid drowning.

In an ill-matched fight involving a male dog of a large breed and a terrier which is in danger of being killed, drastic measures will be necessary and in this case I would not hesitate to kick the big dog between its hind legs – using the instep (not the toe as this would cause cruel permanent injury) but employing enough force to inflict pain severe enough to stop the animal in its tracks. The small dog can then be hastily removed from the scene before the other recovers.

Fights can occur between bitches when one of them is in season and these battles may be serious because they are triggered by sexual excitement. Obviously, this happens only indoors at home (a bitch running loose will be far too busy coping with male admirers), and is a progression from violent play and one bitch mounting another until a member of the party loses her temper. Such battles are prevented by never leaving bitches alone together in this situation.

Biting

With few exceptions Jack Russell terriers are good-natured dogs, not given to biting postmen, although most will protect their homes against genuine intruders with considerable effect. When a dog does take to biting there is usually a reason behind it: apart from mismanagement, a dog that has barked at some stupid delivery man and received a kick in return is liable to turn nasty with any stranger who calls at the house from then on.

Curing a biter which has been justifiably disillusioned by a kick is difficult and sometimes impossible to manage and is one of the most infuriating situations for an owner who takes care to rear puppies to behave correctly. I had an experience of this when an unknown person came into my garden to ask the way to some place in the village. One of my terriers approached him and promptly received a sharp kick in the ribs, whereupon she responded by tearing a hole in the man's trousers and grazing his leg. By this time I had appeared and retrieved the angry dog, and was subjected to a stream of abuse before my visitor left uttering dire threats. One of the nice things about living in an English village is that everyone knows you and your animals. Later that same day a local policeman turned up at my door to tell me that the man had filed a complaint against me and my savage dog. When he heard the true story he told me to forget the matter. 'If you hear any more from that chap, let me know,' he said. The problem was that while I could forget, my dog could not, and she was never again reliable with strangers; this was a nuisance to me during all the remaining years of her life.

On the other side of the coin, an elderly relative of mine had a beloved but most badly behaved smooth-coated Jack Russell named Lucy. This little bitch was reputed to have bitten every one of a population of eight hundred souls in her owner's village, which while of course an exaggeration was not all that far off the mark. The old lady had never made the smallest attempt to discipline her, but in fact she was a sweet dog if you kept within her rules. The principle rule was that no gesture should be made towards her owner: I was bitten through my wrist-watch when I made the mistake of offering the old lady a cup of tea. The reasoning behind Lucy's antisocial behaviour was simple: she was protecting her frail old mistress from attack, and since her owner was both pleased and amused by this attitude, there was no hope of a cure in her case.

However, in normal circumstances, a dog that bites is a serious nuisance and one that may bring its owner up against the law, with the possibility of a court order insisting on the animal's destruction. This is a fair judgment if anybody, and more particularly a child, has been severely bitten without due cause. An acceptable cause would be burglary or an assault upon the owner.

Once a biter, always a biter, is an accurate maxim where terriers are concerned, because the shemozzle caused by the initial attack will have acted as an excitant and all the more so if the bitten person has kicked out in self-defence. This means that prevention has more hope of success than a would-be cure. A puppy should start as it is meant to go on — meeting everyone who calls at the house. While indoors it must learn to stay quietly in its bed when a visitor is present. This early training will prevent a dog defending the house against all comers and eventually taking a bite out of somebody.

Acquired habits

One of the more tiresome habits that can be acquired by a dog is jumping up. This usually starts with a puppy asking to be picked up and fondled, and can be stopped at that stage by always putting it back on its four legs, saying 'No' in a firm voice, and then bending down to pat it.

In a grown dog the habit virtually becomes a reflex action and requires sterner measures. As the dog rears up it should be given a butt in the chest with a knee and told 'No, down!', and if this fails one of its hind feet should be pressed with a toe of a shoe, which will make it drop down immediately because something unseen is happening to its foot. Obviously, the pressure must be a light warning, not a stamp that might cause injury.

Playing tag when called is the result of bad training, often because the dog has come when it was called and been smacked for whatever it was doing before that. If a dog is to be cursed or smacked for a misdeed it must be caught in the act so that it can understand why it is in trouble; otherwise simple logic will tell it that its most recent act was the fault and this is bewildering if that act was to respond obediently to a call. This puts the animal in 'two minds': its first reaction is one of obedience to previous training, but then it remembers that coming to a call last time appeared to be wrong. And so the dog comes just so far and then dodges away for fear of reprisals.

This situation is infuriating for the owner, but it is vital to remain calm and patient or matters will only get worse, as the dog senses anger and becomes more and more nervous, and at a loss as to what to do. Since the owner is at fault, it is up to him or her to convey some form of apology and regain the dog's confidence, and this is begun by sitting or squatting down (to become smaller in the dog's eyes) and ask rather than command it to come – if necessary using some titbit as bait. Every gesture should be slow and the voice gentle until the dog dares to come within reach, when it must be patted and praised.

After the apologetic reunion, it should be allowed to wander away a short distance and then recalled to a warm welcome once again. The objective is to wipe out a bad memory and replace it with a sense of security and friendliness; it may take a while and involve considerable patience, but this is the only means of retrieving a lost rapport between a dog and its owner.

Punishment is a difficult subject. After many years of living with dogs I have concluded that it is never right to hit an animal with the intention of inflicting pain as punishment for a misdeed, because this behaviour is not within a dog's understanding and merely serves to frighten it. The dogs in my home have always either been related to one another or introduced in early puppyhood to become adopted members of that canine family, each with its place in a hierarchy; which has enabled me to watch their behaviour amongst themselves.

There has always been a top dog who maintains control by

force of character rather than by physical violence, and the others respond with varying degrees of submission to a warning growl. One I specially remember was Jerry, a model father who kindly played with his puppies until one over-stepped the mark and became too cheeky, when he would take it by the scruff and give it a shake as a reminder that there were limits to his endurance. The puppy was unharmed but aware that it should mind its manners in future.

I have tried to pattern my behaviour towards the dogs on these observations, replacing a growl with *Ugh* sounds, using the scruff to shake, and a light smack as the alternative to a snap, and have found that this system works far better as a means of general control because the dogs understand me.

Bearing in mind that a loving companion dog is a highly sensitive animal, it must not be allowed to remain in disgrace for long because it will be utterly forlorn. A forgiven dog shakes itself as if to cast off the misery and becomes its normal jolly self again. I somehow arrived at a rather silly arrangement with one of my bitches: when she had done a minor wrong I could say quietly, 'You are a naughty girl, come and have your bottom smacked', and she would stand in front of me, her rear slightly crouched, to receive a token tap on the behind; then shake herself and wag at me as if to say, 'Phew, well that's over and done with!'

Straying and lone hunting

In these days of heavy traffic and intensive farming no dog is safe on its own away from home and a dog owner should consider a properly fenced garden as a priority. Left to himself, a male dog will almost certainly stray around the neighbourhood in search of bitches in season, becoming a traffic hazard and a general nuisance. If he is in the country and seen near lambing ewes or a covert where game-birds are preserved he is liable to be shot or, trapped, or to pick up poisoned baits laid for vermin. Innocence is no safeguard against farmers or gamekeepers who have suffered damage from other dogs. Equally, a wandering dog is likely to mess on pavements or sidewalks and other places, and so add fuel to the fire of the growing number of anti-dog lobbyists who campaign to ban dogs from towns and cities, perhaps forgetting that dogs represent companionship and solace to numbers of otherwise lonely people.

In my experience there is no certain cure for straying males, apart from castration which may work in some cases. The advantage of a bitch is that she is less prone to wandering, unless she is accidentally allowed out when in season. A single dog living in the country is unlikely to go off on lone hunting expeditions, but a pair or several are subject to temptation encouraged by a pack instinct. Accepting the fact that instinct will lead two otherwise well-behaved dogs to go off in search of rabbits or foxes, and that no amount of cursing and smacking will stop them once they have tasted the excitement of the chase, the only solution is prevention by means of a good fence, its base let into the ground to deter digging under. People who lose beloved dogs and are left to imagine what may have happened to them, whether they have been strangled by a wire snare or trapped by the collar in a badgers' sett to die of starvation, will appreciate the value of a fence.

Livestock worrying

The one crime that a Jack Russell terrier is unlikely to commit is chasing sheep or cattle, its natural interest is in finding burrows by searching along ditches and hedgerows and among undergrowth in woodlands. It may be led astray, however, in a mixed pack of other breeds if it is allowed to run free with them. It is up to the owner to prevent this, because although a small dog may be allowed one bite at a human being, a charge of sheep worrying might bring a court order condemning it to death.

9

Accidents and Ailments

The Jack Russell terrier is a hardy dog and, on the whole, less liable to disease than some other pedigree breeds; in recent years some of these have become prone to hereditary malformations and diseases largely due to inbreeding for show points. Now that Jack Russells have gained the limelight as attractive companion dogs it is vitally important for breeders to ensure that no stud dogs or brood bitches carrying inheritable defects are used for breeding, because only in this way can the breed maintain its reputation for sturdiness and longevity.

The incidence of hereditary hip dysplasia, progressive retinal atrophy, and congenital cataract, is so rare in Jack Russells that these problems are virtually unknown, but an inherited weakness known as slipped stifle might become a problem if it is not watched.

Hereditary diseases

Slipped Stifle
This can be described as the dislocation of the kneecap in a hind leg. It occurs in miniature poodles, the smaller terrier breeds and in toy dogs.

Symptoms: the dog is seen to be carrying one hind leg, usually after exercise. The joint may be painful. The dislocation can be manipulated back into place by a vet but is liable to recur without surgical treatment. It is important to obtain a true diagnosis to discover if there is a fundamental fault in the joint to indicate hereditary slipped stifle since the trouble could be the result of a fall on rough ground and nothing more than that. If there is a fault the dog must not breed.

Hernia

The usual forms are *inguinal* in bitches, *scrotal* in dogs, and *umbilical* in either sex.

Symptoms: inguinal hernia appears as a raised patch or small lump under the skin inside the hind leg where it joins the belly. It is probably harmless but should be seen by a vet to confirm this. Scrotal hernia is seen in dog puppies as an enlargement, usually at one side, of the scrotum and almost certainly needs minor surgery. Umbilical hernia is common in young puppies, appearing as a small lump on the navel, in most cases caused by a slight rupture which allows a small portion of fat to protrude. If the lump is small it is likely to disappear after a time without any ill effect, but it must be watched to make sure that it does not increase in size; if it does it must receive veterinary treatment. Some strains within a breed are more susceptible to hernias than others, but as it is a comparatively harmless defect it should not necessarily preclude breeding from animals which are otherwise sound.

Cramp

This may occur in dogs given unaccustomed violent exercise, but a tendency to cramp can be inbred into a strain which has been created by mating closely related animals.

Symptoms: in the midst of running a dog collapses, often crying out in pain, with the body rigidly cramped until the spasm passes. At first sight these symptoms could be mistaken for a heart attack or fit, but in the former the gums would be bluish and in the latter the dog is unconscious, whereas anybody who has suffered from cramp knows that one is all too aware of the pain. Cramp should not be taken as hereditary in Jack Russells unless it appears in succeeding generations of related dogs; if it does, a programme of complete outcross matings with totally unrelated dogs will stamp it out.

Monorchid and Cryptorchid

These terms describe a male dog in which only one testicle has descended into the scrotum. The fault is inheritable and such animals should not be used for breeding. It is a wise precaution to arrange for a vet to carry out surgical removal of the undescended testicle which may otherwise become cancerous in later life.

Virus diseases

Five major killer diseases affect dogs. These are canine distemper, hardpad, virus hepatitis, leptospiral jaundice and canine parvovirus. Fortunately the first four are prevented in at least 90 per cent of cases by a combined vaccine given in two inoculations about two weeks apart after a puppy has been finally weaned from its dam's milk for a period of a month. The simple injections are given by a vet who will provide a card detailing the animal's name, the dates of the injections, the diseases covered by the vaccination and when booster inoculation is advisable. He will also advise on when the vaccine may be considered to have taken effect, which will be about ten days after the second injection; it is important not to allow a puppy in public places until this time has elapsed. Sometimes a busy vet forgets to mention this last and vital inoculation, leaving a novice owner under the impression that after one prick of the needle the dog is 100 per cent safe. As an example of this, I met an acquaintance exercising a very small puppy on a grass patch beside the car park in a local town. I could not resist saying, 'Forgive me, but you really are being unwise. The grass here might be full of disease'. She replied, 'Oh, it's quite safe. He's just been up to the vet for his injection.'

Since the development of vaccines, and a growing public awareness of the importance of inoculation, the incidence of distemper and the related but deadlier virus hardpad, and of hepatitis and leptospirosis, has diminished to a remarkable extent. But this does not mean that dog owners should be complacent, because outbreaks still flare up occasionally. For this reason it is as well to know the major symptoms.

Jack Russells enjoy learning a few tricks and were often used in circus acts until poodles bacame popular. At one time, no Punch and Judy show was complete without a bored terrier wearing a ruff, sitting at the side of the stage (*Panther Photographic International*)

South East Jack Russell Club race meeting at Farncombe, Surrey

This cat has reared two
orphaned Jack Russell
puppies with her own kitten.
Dogs and cats can become
lifelong friends if they are
introduced at an early age

This eager pup will not be
easily diverted from the object
of its attention

Distemper and hardpad

Distemper and hardpad symptoms are similar to those in human gastric flu: there is fever with a temperature of 40·5C (105F) or more; there is discharge from eyes and nose, and diarrhoea. A characteristic musty smell is often present in the dog. Only prompt veterinary treatment, careful nursing and slow convalescence will save an affected animal, but unfortunately survivors of hardpad may suffer from brain damage, resulting in chorea (St Vitus' Dance) which is incurable.

Virus hepatitis and leptospiral jaundice

Virus hepatitus (or Rubarth's disease) and leptospiral jaundice (Stuttgart disease) both have symptoms of jaundice in later stages, but first show as gastro-enteritis. The dog is obviously seriously ill with a high fever, and in the case of hyperacute hepatitis may die very suddenly, without any sign of disease.

All these diseases are contagious, which means that dogs contract them by sniffing where other dogs have been. An apparently fit dog which has survived a mild attack of hepatitis may remain a 'carrier' for life. Leptospirosis is not strictly a virus but an organism known as *spirochaete*, but as it is included in comprehensive vaccines it may be considered as such. It is a serious menace to owners of Jack Russell terriers because it is carried by some 50 per cent of a given population of rats, and so any dog that is likely to take part in rat hunts, or indeed sniff about where rats run, must be given regular booster injections.

Canine parvovirus

Canine parvovirus hit the dog population of Britain towards the end of 1978, after having been known for a while longer in the USA and Australia. Since it was a new disease, dogs were totally susceptible and the result was a frightening epidemic with a high mortality rate.

Urgent research in America, Australia, and Britain indicated that the virus was an aberrant form of infectious feline enteritis, but distinct and not transmitted from one species to the other. It attacks dogs of all ages with symptoms of high fever, vomiting and blood-stained diarrhoea; the mortality rate in a litter of puppies may be as high as 100 per cent and heart damage is a common complication.

In the early stages of the outbreak, feline enteritis vaccine (FEV) was used as a protective measure with some success, but vaccines specifically for canine parvovirus are now available and a vet will advise on the latest and most successful.

Owners must realise that this new disease is highly contagious, transmitted from all the bodily excretions of an infected animal, and so it is only common sense to ensure that dogs are given the appropriate inoculations.

Rabies

Rabies has not been a problem in Britain since a stringent quarantine law was introduced in the 1920s, and the same applies in Australia and New Zealand where importation laws are enforced with equal firmness. But, because the world grows smaller as travel becomes faster and easier, it is as well to understand the facts of the disease rather than its mythology.

Rabies exists to a greater or lesser extent in Europe, the Middle East, Africa, the whole of Asia and in North and South America. Contrary to common belief, dogs are not the prime vectors of rabies, but intermediaries between rabid wild animals and man – a wandering dog may be bitten by an infected fox to become rabid itself and then bite a human being and so pass on the dread virus. Research has shown that foxes are the main source in Europe and Canada, while skunks head the list in the USA and vampire bats in South America. These countries rely on vaccination as the best preventative measure for dogs; but Britain disagrees, largely because vaccination certificates could be forged, or outwardly healthy dogs allowed into the country with a certificate might, in fact, be carriers.

The disease is transmitted from saliva, either into a bite or into a graze or scratch on the skin. A human being who is bitten by an animal suspected of rabies can be saved by a course of fourteen progressively more painful injections of antiserum over a period of two weeks. At the present time, there is no treatment available for a previously unvaccinated dog that has been bitten, which underlines the importance of vaccination for dogs living in countries where rabies is endemic – indeed, this is compulsory in some of them.

Skin parasites and diseases

Fleas are the commonest active skin parasites, with lice second; ticks and harvest mites are found only on dogs living in the country. The first two can be eradicated by using an insecticidal powder or shampoo specifically made for animal treatment. *Never* use a product containing DDT because this is poisonous to all animals.

Fleas

These are readily seen among the hair of a smooth-coated terrier, but the only sign of infestation in a broken or rough coat may be that the dog scratches and nibbles its skin. When the hair is parted fleas will be seen scurrying in all directions, the young being black and the adult specimens a dull brown.

Treatment involves working the powder or shampoo into the hair, starting behind the ears and ending with the tail and hindquarters, so that the fleas are prevented from taking refuge on the dog's head. It is important to avoid the eyes and interior of the ears, and powdering should be done outdoors facing into the wind so that particles are not inhaled. Fleas lay eggs which hatch on the dog within ten days and so treatment must be repeated at that time to ensure complete eradication.

At the same time a dog's blanket should be washed to remove any eggs adhering to it, and if the house has fitted carpets it is worth powdering under the edges, because fleas may deposit eggs there too, if the room is warm. Flea collars are on the market and some people find them reasonably efficient, but because they are impregnated with an insecticide I would not leave one on a dog for longer than three weeks at a time, while keeping a constant watch that the skin of the neck does not become inflamed.

Lice

An itchy dog which does not appear to have fleas may have lice. These are harder to find in the hair, but examination (perhaps with the help of a magnifying glass) will show clusters of minute greyish creatures, usually along the spine/and on the chest. A thorough bathing with insecticidal shampoo will remove them.

Ticks

Dogs pick up ticks while running about on grassland grazed by sheep or rabbits. A tick first appears as a small dark crab-like creature, but once it has selected a place and buried its head in the dog's skin, it swells to resemble a grey pea. Removing ticks should be done with care because if they are pulled off the head may be left in the skin to create an abscess. It can be induced to release its hold with a drop of undiluted antiseptic, such as Dettol, but I use a lighted cigarette on the top of the 'pea' and then remove the creature with tweezers. It should then be burned or flushed down a drain.

In parts of France and Italy, and in some other countries, these parasites carry *tick fever*. This serious disease is caused by an organism injected into a dog when it is bitten by the host tick.

Harvest mites (Chiggers)

These parasites are also picked up in the countryside and resemble microscopic ticks. They commonly fasten on to a dog's feet, often between the toes, to cause angry spots and violent itching. An ammonia solution is the best treatment for mites on the feet, but this should be done only in consultation with a vet. Harvest mites occasionally enter a dog's ear to give rise to symptoms of 'canker' (see below).

Mites are also responsible for three forms of mange found on dogs: *sarcoptic* (red mange), *follicular* (black mange), and *otodectic* (ear mange). Both red and ear mange are highly infectious and may be passed from dog to dog by physical contact or from kennel walls and bedding, but these forms respond well to modern treatment given under veterinary supervision. Black mange is less infectious but often proves difficult to cure.

116

Any dog which shows signs of bald patches, either scaly or inflamed, should be examined at once by a vet, who may need to take a skin scraping for analysis under a miscroscope in order to discover whether the cause is one of the manges, or possibly ring worm or dry eczema which can appear similar in the early stages.

Ringworm

This is not a parasite but a fungus. It is transmitted from dog to dog and also from buildings and woodwork which has been rubbed against by infected cattle up to six months previously. Prompt treatment is required and modern drugs will effect a cure within a short time, but meanwhile it is essential to find the source of the infection and to keep the dog isolated. The first sign is a circular (hence 'ring') scaly patch, often on the head, which is intensely itchy, and if this is left untreated more patches will appear and spread to join up and leave large areas of bald encrusted skin on the miserable sufferer. I have had experience of ringworm only once, when one of my Jack Russells killed a huge rat which (to my horror) I saw was covered in it; within a week a patch appeared on the dog's cheek.

Eczema

The eruptions on the skin caused by eczema may be in one of two forms: 'wet eczema' is seen as a moist patch which is surrounded by an area of greasy hair that falls away to enlarge the patch. Such areas are both itchy and painful. Exterior treatment involves washing the part gently and then applying an antibiotic powder. 'Dry eczema' is so easily confused with mange and ringworm that veterinary diagnosis is vital.

Eczema is not a skin disease as such but a symptom of internal disorders, often aggravated by hot humid weather, and usually traceable to an incorrect diet. A reduction in starch, an increase in animal protein and the addition of vitamin B in the diet are usually all that is needed to prevent a further outbreak.

Blane ('Nettle Rash')

This can be caused by insect bites or nettle stings, but more often it appears on dogs that are overweight and subjected to sudden exercise; or it can be caused by a digestive upset. In severe cases the head and ears may puff-up, but the common symptoms are a few lumps and bumps on the back and flanks. Sponging with lukewarm water provides some relief, and the dog may be given a pinch of baking soda (bicarbonate of soda) in a spoonful of cold water. Blane almost always appears only in hot humid weather.

'Riff'

This ailment seems to be better known to terrier breeders than to the veterinary profession, and is the subject of some controversy. As far as I know it affects only predominantly white-haired terriers with broken or rough coats, including wire-haired fox terriers and, of course, Jack Russells. The symptoms are straightforward enough for an owner to diagnose: an affected dog constantly nibbles at the skin on the insides of its front legs from the armpits down to the toes and the skin appears to exude a pinkish moisture which stains the hair pink, possibly when it is mixed with the nibbler's saliva.

Various views are expressed on the subject of riff, blaming it on anything from lack of kennel hygiene to harvest mites and eczema. In my opinion it is none of these and is more likely to be the result of some form of allergy, possibly related to sunlight, since the trouble normally arises in the spring, continues through the summer and then subsides with the approach of winter; in fact, it may be a type of sunburn. Whatever the cause, in the single case that has affected one of my own terriers, a Jack Russell X West Highland white, I found that washing the front legs with warm water and a mild bathroom soap alleviated the itching and even cured the trouble for some time. Sunburn lotion must *not* be used, as the dog might be poisoned by licking the treated part.

Worms

The danger to humanity, especially children, of canine worms is a subject beloved by the media. In fact, there is a better chance of winning a national lottery than there is of suffering ill effects from parasitic worms transmitted by puppies and dogs. However, that does not mean that worms are harmless to dogs and should not be taken seriously.

The roundworm (*Toxocara canis*) found in puppies will, if left untreated, stunt their growth and, if present in large numbers, even kill them. An adult dog infested with tapeworms will suffer from malnutrition because the worms eat what the dog eats. Puppies should be treated against roundworm as a routine measure; but dogs should not be dosed for tapeworms unless it is certain that these parasites are present with segments of them appearing in the droppings. Details of worming procedures are given in Chapter 2.

Injuries

Jack Russell terriers which are involved in country sports are liable to wounds of various kinds, especially tears in the skin from barbed wire. Minor cuts of this nature should be swabbed with a solution of Dettol or TCP or similar antiseptic and then treated with an antibiotic powder. If a wound is large enough to require stitching by a vet it should not be given any home treatment as this will delay the vet, who has first to clean away any powder or ointment.

A fox seldom attacks a terrier unless it is cornered and the dog goes in too close, but the badger is a much braver animal, inclined to charge a dog and inflict terrible bites in its throat and chest. Any bite, including those received in a fight with another dog, must be treated seriously because punctures through the skin to the underlying muscle can inject dirt and bacteria which may result in a deep-seated ulcer – particularly if the skin is allowed to heal too quickly. A vet will inject an antibiotic and advise on treatment.

An injury which includes profuse bleeding needs urgent attention. If blood is pulsing a tourniquet must be used, which can be made by knotting a handkerchief into a loop and tightening it with the aid of a stick or pencil; but it must be remembered that a tourniquet has to be released at intervals of *not more than twenty minutes*, because cutting off the blood supply to a part for longer than this will achieve permanent damage and a danger of gangrene. It is only feasible to use a tourniquet on a limb. Bleeding from the throat or body can be partially controlled by pinching the lips of the wound between finger and thumb until professional help arrives.

Sometimes a superficial wound will bleed copiously, particularly if it is in an ear, and then clotting may be encouraged by applying an ice cube wrapped in a clean cloth, but *do not* use ice if the dog is in shock; it must be kept warm in that case.

Dogs which have been involved in a traffic accident may have fractured limbs or internal injuries. A vet will treat broken bones according to the extent of the injury: a simple fracture may need only a plaster cast kept in place for about three weeks, but more complicated cases necessitate an operation to plate or pin the bone.

Internal injury can be suspected if the gums turn whitish, but this is no certain diagnosis because shock can produce the same effect. The worried owner of a badly injured dog must realise that the animal is extremely frightened, all the more so as primeval instinct will tell it that crippling spells death, and so it is important to remain calm and to soothe and reassure the dog while waiting for the vet and during subsequent treatment.

Bandaging

Minor wounds are best left uncovered to heal, but it may be necessary to bandage a cut foot or leg to keep the part clean when the dog is outdoors. Always use three layers: first lint, second cottonwool and third crêpe (elasticated) bandage, so that the dressing is well padded and not liable to restrict circulation, which can happen if a cotton bandage is tied too tightly. It is better not to split the end of a bandage to give two ends to knot together, as this attracts chewing by the patient. Instead the end should be held in place with a strip of sticking plaster. In wet weather a plastic bag can be fitted over the bandaged part, again held with sticking plaster or sticky tape, but this must be removed after the dog has been out.

Canker

Canker is an old-fashioned term still in common use as a description of a number of ear disorders. A dog that shows symptoms of earache by scratching and shaking its head should be examined by a vet, who can diagnose the trouble with the aid of an auroscope and prescribe suitable treatment. 'Canker' must not be neglected, because not only is it very painful to the animal but it may be the first signs of otodectic mange. Other causes are harvest mites, eczema, excess wax, inflammation caused by damp, and the presence of a foreign body such as a grass seed. *Never* probe the ear.

Anal glands

These glands are part of a dog's scent mechanism, used for territorial marking in association with urine and glands in the hind feet which function when a dog scrapes the ground after it has relieved itself. There are two anal glands, found inside the anus; they normally cover the droppings in a musky secretion as they are passed. Occasionally these glands become blocked and impacted, giving rise to a painful condition which either prevents the dog from evacuating its bowels or causes it to howl with pain when it attempts to do so. A sign, sometimes mistaken for worms, is that the dog skates its rear along the ground, which it does because this ailment is intensely itchy in the early stages.

A vet will treat the trouble by squeezing out the impacted material, but it is liable to recur at intervals unless there is some alteration in the diet, because in most cases the cause is that the droppings are too soft to stimulate the action of the glands. Regular roughage in the form of lightly cooked green vegetables, including the stems, and beef shin bones which can be ground (not splintered) by gnawing, will go a long way towards preventing a recurrence of impaction.

121

Mammary tumours

Jack Russell bitches seem particularly prone to these tumours in middle and old age. The first symptom is a pea-sized lump under or near a teat, which may grow into one large lump or proliferate into several small ones. Most of these tumours are more or less malignant but often are so slow-growing that a dog may reach the end of her days before surgery is necessary. However, even a small lump should be examined by a vet, and monitored at intervals, because if surgical removal becomes necessary this is a simple operation provided that the cancer has not spread. A common site in terrier bitches is in the teats on the chest and I suspect that this may be caused in the first place by superficial damage while she is digging in a borrow.

Poisoning

Deadly poisons are easily available on the shelves of garden shops and hardware stores. Among the most dangerous are weedkillers containing paraquat, slug pellets and warfarin rat bait, yet none of these products is marketed with sufficient warnings about its potentially lethal nature. Who reads the small print on a label? All these, and strychnine laid in baits for vermin, kill innumerable dogs every year.

Dogs can pick up paraquat while eating weed grasses. There is no known antidote for human beings, let alone animals. But from a dog's point of view slug pellets, rat poison and strychnine are more dangerous because they are given an attractive taste.

Treatment: a dog suspected of having eaten a poison must be rushed to a vet's surgery while someone else telephones to give details so that an antidote may be prepared pending its arrival; but an owner should realise that the prospects for saving the animal are minimal unless it has taken only a small amount. If delay is unavoidable, perhaps because of a long car journey to the surgery, the dog should be given an emetic so that the contents of the stomach are vomited, thus reducing the amount of poison absorbed into the system. The best emetic is a lump of washing-soda the size of a hazel nut given as a pill, but failing this a heaped teaspoonful of common salt diluted in a little warm water will act almost as well.

It is vital *not* to give milk or any other oily liquid if there is doubt as to whether a dog may have taken a phosphorous poison, because this would accelerate its deadly effect.

Toad poisoning

The common toad can secrete a mild venom if it is picked up by an inquisitive dog. This is seldom, if ever, fatal but can produce some alarming symptoms. The dog vomits repeatedly, slavers ropy saliva and may become briefly unconscious.

Snake-bite

Britain has only one poisonous snake, the adder or viper, which lives in woodland and on the moors. I have spent most of my life in a part of England where adders are common but none of my dogs has been bitten in spite of several encounters. A bite is usually the result of an accident; a terrier busy in search of rabbits may disturb an adder which bites in defence. The gape of an adder's jaws is comparatively small, which means its fangs can inject venom only into a limb on a dog, or into a human hand.

A bitten dog suffers pain and swelling in that area, plus vomiting, convulsions and collapse, with a faint heartbeat. Immediate first aid involves putting a tourniquet above the bite to prevent the poison spreading, incising the site to promote bleeding and then packing the cut as deeply as possible with permanganate of potash crystals. The dog may be given strong coffee or a little brandy to encourage the heart while it is kept as quiet and warm as possible until veterinary help is obtained.

The same treatment applies in America and other countries where dangerous snakes are common. Anyone exercising a dog where poisonous snakes are known to abound would be wise to carry a small quantity of permanganate of potash crystals, a sharp knife and a length of material which may be used as a ligature in an emergency.

Ailments of a bitch and her litter

Giving birth and suckling a litter is a natural function and the average bitch benefits both physically and mentally from this experience. However, just occasionally things go wrong and so she needs watching for any symptoms that suggest all is not well.

Metritis (inflammation of the uterus)

It is normal for a bitch to show a certain amount of discharge for a day or so after whelping, but if the discharge is foetid and she appears unwell, off her food and feverish, and has little or no milk, then prompt veterinary attention is vital. The cause may be a dead foetus, a retained afterbirth or some internal injury.

Mastitis

Inflammation of the teat may appear at any time during the suckling period. The usual first sign is that the bitch will lie down to feed her litter and then get up almost immediately because they are causing her pain. Examination will show that one or more of the teats is hot and tender. If the trouble is not spotted early, she will become feverish and off her food. A vet will prescribe antibiotic treatment but the problem is that drugs given to the bitch will be transmitted to her puppies via her milk, which can result in a fading litter. Vitamin B and other extra vitamins appear to offset this danger to some degree.

In most cases mastitis can be traced to a lack of hygiene: dirt can be injected into the teat by the claws of a suckling pup if the whelping bed and the area around it are not kept clean, or the bitch herself may go to feed them when her chest and belly has a splattering of mud from a farm or stable yard. Therefore, prevention is a matter of cleanliness and clipping the *tips* of the puppies' claws.

Eclampsia (Milk Fever)

A Jack Russell terrier bitch is less likely to suffer from milk fever than breeds which have large litters because it is caused by a lack of calcium in her body following heavy lactation (it is common in deep-milking dairy cows). There should be no fear of it if a bitch has received a nourishing diet during the gestation and lactation periods but, all the same, the symptoms are worth knowing because of the chance that it might happen.

The symptoms of milk fever are frightening: the bitch staggers and then goes down in a fit, her legs outstretched and head thrown back, the body shivering violently. Prompt veterinary treatment is of the utmost importance, because without it a bitch will die after a succession of spasms culminating in heart failure. A vet will give an intravenous injection of calcium borogluconate solution which, if there has been no delay, should produce an almost immediate recovery, and he will then advise on the necessary aftercare of the bitch and her puppies.

Fading Litters
The advent of parvovirus has meant that losses among newborn puppies has increased. Other reasons include canine herpes, hepatitis, a disparity in the parental blood groups and hypothermia. The common symptom is that the litter fails to suckle and the puppies crawl about the nest uttering characteristic mewing cries until they weaken and die. Since puppies in this condition are certainly going to die anyway, it may be necessary for a vet to sacrifice one for post-mortem examination so that the cause can be identified, when there may be some hope of saving the rest. The sole blame for a case of hypothermia rests with the owner; no bitch and her litter can be kept in cold, draughty quarters.

Destruction of Unwanted Puppies
It sometimes happens that a puppy is born malformed or is damaged while or immediately after being born and has to be humanely destroyed. Nobody likes doing this to a helpless little animal which has just arrived in the world, but it must be done, quickly and without causing pain or distress. Sentimental people sometimes advocate drowning such newborn puppies in a bucket of warm water, evidently on the principle that warm water will not be as nasty as cold water when it comes to

drowning. In fact the warmth will delay death, whereas ice-cold water will cause almost immediate heart failure. However, in my view, it is the duty of the owner to give a damaged puppy instantaneous oblivion, and the only way to achieve this is with a hard blow on the head: the puppy should be held in one hand with the head resting on a solid surface (such as a brick) and the skull is then given a sharp blow with a heavy stick or length of metal piping. This form of destruction is permissible for up to twenty-four hours after birth, but puppies older than this *must* be taken to a vet, who will inject a fatal dose of a barbiturate drug.

General information

Here are some general notes on your Jack Russell's health:

Normal temperature is 38·5C (101·5F). To check blood temperature use a blunt-ended clinical thermometer, greased with vaseline, and insert it in the rectum.

Pulse: the rate is between 70 and 100 per minute, but a normally erratic beat requires an expert to diagnose any fault.

Respiration: normal rate is 15–25 per minute.

Teeth: the milk teeth begin to erupt from the gums of a puppy when it is three weeks old; it has a complete set of twenty-eight when it is about six weeks old. These are replaced by forty-two permanent teeth from about four months onwards. Sometimes an upper canine ('eye' tooth) grows up beside the milk-tooth version which fails to fall out as it should. In most instances the provision of beef bones and other safe chewy objects will loosen the tooth and put matters right.

Urine samples: a urine sample may be required so that a vet can use it to diagnose some ailment. The best receptacle is a spare saucer, which must be thoroughly washed and rinsed. The dog is taken out on a lead and when he or she urinates the saucer can be slipped underneath to collect a specimen equivalent to about one tablespoonful, which is then poured into an equally clean bottle.

Giving medicine: if a dog is to receive any form of treatment, show it what is to be done, rather than using force, unless this is absolutely necessary. A trusting companion dog will accept a powder or ointment on a sore place if it is first allowed to sniff the stuff, while being reassured with kind words. The same applies to liquid medicines to be given by mouth: first allow a sniff, then kneel behind the sitting dog, lift its lip at one side and pour in the measured dose – a little at a time if the amount is more than a teaspoonful (5ml) to avoid choking. The easiest way to give a tablet is to hide it in a small piece of butter, soft cheese or meat, which the dog will accept as a titbit. Otherwise, again show the tablet and work from the rear of the sitting dog, opening its jaws by pressure of the fingers of one hand while placing the tablet as far back as possible behind its tongue. Some dogs are crafty about holding a pill and spitting it out just when you think it has been swallowed. In this case, hold the muzzle gently but firmly closed with a thumb across the nostrils, and then stroke the dog's throat.

10

The Terrier and the
Rev John Russell

While hounds of various kinds can be traced back for several thousand years, written or pictorial records of terriers in historic times are few. Since virtually all working terriers originated in the British Isles, it may be that one of the earliest types is represented by a skeleton dating from c 1750 BC which was excavated from an Early Bronze Age site at Windmill Hill, near the monoliths at Avebury and not far from Stonehenge in Southern England. All that can be said of these bones is that they are the remains of a small dog of fox-terrier size.

By the time Julius Caesar arrived in 55 BC there were a number of indigenous dogs, including huge mastiffs and a small breed of hound which was later described by the poet-historian Oppian:

... 'Are beagles called, and to the chase are led;
Their bodies small and of so mean a shape,
You'd think them curs that under tables gape.'

This scholar's translation is justified because the name beagle comes from the Celtic *beag* (Welsh *bach*), meaning small, which was corrupted in medieval England to *brach*, a name given to small working dogs that were not curs.

When hunting became the sport of kings in the eleventh century, Canute laid down forest laws of a savage nature, involving the mutilation of larger dogs owned by peasants. The

Norman succession enlarged upon these laws, allowing only sheepdogs or dogs small enough to be passed through an iron ring 7 inches in diameter; all other non-Royal dogs were crippled by being ham-strung or by having the toes of one front foot chopped off. 'Smalle houndes' (beagles) were excluded from these laws.

Forest laws generally applied to deer and wild boar, but otters and hares were also considered important quarry: indeed, the hare was described as 'the king of all venery'. Towards the end of the twelfth century Kings' Otter Hunter was a royal appointment; some two hundred years later Guillaume Twici, huntsman to Edward II, wrote the first known treatise about hunting in England and listed hare, hart (deer), otter, boar, wolf and fox in descending order of precedence.

Clearly, otter and fox hunting needed terriers to bolt the quarry and their existence is proved in the first printed book about rural sports, dated 1486 and attributed to Dame Julyana Berners, an English prioress. In it she lists 'the namys of houndes. First ther is a Grehownd, a Bastard, a Mengrell, a Mastyfe, a Lemor, a Spanyell. Rachys. Kennettys. Teroures. Bocheris houndes. Myddyng dogges. Tryndel-tayles. And Prikherid curris. And smale ladies popis that beere a Way the flees.'

Since there was no standardised spelling, 'Teroures' is also spelt as 'Terrares'; and the alternative usage of dog for hound, and *vice versa*, later caused some confusion. But this book does firmly establish terriers as a type of dog known in England for at least five hundred years.

The hunting scene changed little until the late seventeenth century when wild boar and wolves reached the brink of extinction (the last wolf was killed in the mid-1700s), and foxhunting became fashionable. Within the next hundred years several types of terrier became known in different parts of the British Isles: the cairn is probably the archetypal terrier of Scotland; Border and Lakeland terriers were developed in the North of England; while in the Midlands, Wales and Southern England the commonest types were broken-coated black-and-tans, and white terriers, some pied with lemon or tan markings and either smooth or broken-coated. Among those of the last type was a strain of Devonshire terrier owned by the Rev John Russell senior (father of Parson Jack), in the 1780s.

The first named portrait of a predominantly white terrier with coloured marking was painted in 1796 and shows a dog named Viper. He must have been valued to warrant a painting, but in modern eyes appears an unattractive dog: long-legged and bull-necked, with ears cropped short; perhaps better adapted to fighting contests than to facing a quarry underground.

In 1806 Delabeare P. Blaine, an eminent vet and authority on the diseases of horses and dogs, began the mammoth task of writing his *Encyclopaedia of Rural Sports* which was eventually published in 1840. The section devoted to hunting consists of material which suggests that it was written at the beginning of the century: Scottish and northern terriers in general are described more from hearsay than knowledge, because the author lived in the South of England and terrier types were localised according to the work required of them. On the subject of beagles he mentions several types and the terrier beagle in particular: 'a very hardy and altogether a vermin loving breed'. No sportsman then or now would ever describe the hare as vermin and this leads me to suppose that these broken-coated beagles were in fact part-bred terriers which bequeathed their hound marking to later generations of Jack Russells and fox terriers.

Terriers in the nineteenth century

The nineteenth century was an era of change in many respects and pedigree dog breeding was no exception. There was an upsurge of interest in producing breeds rather than types and this was applied to working terriers in particular, based on a size suited to going to ground with enough courage to face a fierce quarry.

Breeders had two coat types, smooth and broken-coated, and four basic colours to work on. The smooth coat has remained unchanged in the modern fox terrier and in the Jack Russell, but the true broken coat is now found only in border terriers and in Jack Russells: it is midway between the smooth and the profuse wire-hair of the two fox-terrier breeds, and rather shorter than the coats of cairns and Norwich terriers.

The coat pattern usually described as 'grizzle' is probably the original terrier colour. It consists of hairs of two or more colours, some individually banded, which produce a 'pepper and salt' effect; there are grey grizzles (mixed black and white), and others described as wheaten or reddish (yellow/tan/red and white mixed). This sort of pattern is known to geneticists as 'agouti', having taken as a representative the South American rodent of that name, and it is of interest because an animal with agouti colouring is capable of producing offspring of other colours from recessive genes, such as white and black, and further breeding from blacks can result in red coats or may be diluted to appear slate or steel blue.

It is generally agreed that the cairn is the root stock from which all terriers in Scotland descend, including the West Highland white and the Scottish terrier. Some white puppies occurred in litters bred from old strains of cairns in the first half of the nineteenth century, and these were usually destroyed as being useless until a Col E. D. Malcolm of Poltalloch in Argyll decided to select these puppies and breed from them. He took care to establish a type suited to working in the terrain of the Highlands and thus became the pioneer of West Highland whites, a terrier showing a family likeness to the cairn but with a broader head, longer legs and a cobbier build. Another offshoot of the cairn is the Scottish terrier, formerly known as the Aberdeen, in which the commonest colour is black.

Black and tan is a pattern that has been known for centuries in terriers and several other breeds of dog. It is a mutation of agouti which tends to become dominant when it occurs in the course of breeding certain domesticated animals (it is unknown in the wild), and is a distinct oddity: only dogs and fancy rabbits and mice have been bred with this pattern and it does not occur in tame rats or guinea-pigs (cavies).

131

The old broken-coated black-and-tan terrier was of the classic tan pattern: that is, whole black with tan markings on the cheeks, eyebrows, legs and under the tail. A smooth version was bred in the North of England, probably by means of crosses with the Old English white terrier which was smooth-coated; in common with the original Yorkshire terrier, it used to kill rats in matches between a pair of dogs to see which could destroy a specified number confined in a pit in the shortest time. This was a popular sport among miners, who wagered on the results and took great pride in their dogs.

Other black-and-tan-marked terriers were bred in the English Border counties and in Wales, but differed in having a tan body marked with a black saddle. Working terriers in the Lake District of England varied in type and colour and were known by local names, including the Patterdale which still works with most of the hunts in the area and might be mistaken for a cross between a Scottish terrier and a Jack Russell – which it is not. Hunting in mountainous fell country is literally a matter of running up hill and down dale, following on foot a racy breed of hound in pursuit of a fox which appears to be a sub-species: greyish in colour, larger and built on the lines of a greyhound, and with a wolfish taste for lambs. If one of these foxes goes to ground a terrier is sent in either to bolt it or to fight and kill it, because there can be no digging-out when the 'earth' is a hole among rocky crags. This type of powerful and courageous terrier is the ancestor of the modern Lakeland.

Welsh terriers show a superficial resemblance to Lakelands but have a stockier build, weighing about 20lb, and a more phlegmatic character than many other terrier breeds. They have been carefully bred since the mid-eighteenth century, which alone makes them unusual since the majority of dogs were bred in a very haphazard fashion for another hundred years.

On the other side of England, in East Anglia, a distinct type of terrier was used to work against foxes and badgers and these became known as Norwich terriers in the 1870s. It is commonly believed that these dogs were bred from Irish terriers crossed with other working types, but this idea seems to be based on the fact that the most popular colour is red, although black-and-tans, red grizzles and grizzle-and-tans occur. It is a small breed, usually about 10in high and weighing about 12lb, with a harsh wiry coat, and both its appearance and demeanour suggest that in all probability it is a product of crosses between cairns and the old sporting Yorkshire terrier; it is a keen worker but not a fighter, and is very affectionate by nature. Two types existed: one with prick ears and the other with drop ears, which are now known as Norwich and Norfolk terriers respectively and bred separately.

The rise and fall of the sealyham terrier

The sealyham is of interest to breeders of Jack Russell terriers because both were developed during the nineteenth century for a specific purpose: the first by Capt John Edwardes and the second by the Rev John Russell, almost certainly unknown to each other but working in parallel, give or take a few years, and achieving very similar results during their lifetimes.

Capt Edwardes was born in 1808 and, sharing Russell's longevity, died in 1891. He inherited the Sealyham estate in South Wales and retired from the army in the 1840s to live there and soon established a pack of otter hounds and began breeding terriers of a standardised type from predominantly white dogs of unrecorded origins. His objective was to produce a small, game and active terrier; agile enough to work in rocky, often precipitous country, and of a size capable of entering an otter's holt, which meant a maximum weight of 16lb and a preference for those of 14lb.

Not surprisingly, the result was a facsimile of the old '14/14' Jack Russell terrier, which is clearly seen in photographs of early sealyhams, such as Duck, a foundation bitch which was rather leggy with a broken coat and dark patches on the head and back. She was matched with a shorter-legged dog named Brass Bach, an evidently dominant sire as succeeding generations were shorter in the leg and similar to the modern broken-coated Jack Russell.

133

When Capt Edwardes died his terriers were dispersed and a number earned fame for their courage in the 'sport' of badger digging and baiting. The breed first appeared at a recognised show in 1910 and became immediately popular as companions and show dogs, reaching a peak in Britain and North America between the two World Wars, by which time sealyhams had been altered to become too bulky and heavy to be considered as working dogs. The standard now required a dog not more than 12in in height and weighing up to 20lb. Some strains gave the breed as a whole a bad reputation for fighting and owners of companion dogs found that the sealyham's profuse white coat and short legs made it difficult to keep clean and well-groomed, and it was then on a downward path.

After World War II interest in the breed was kept alive by Sir Jocelyn Lucas, whose Ilmer kennel gained worldwide recognition, not because his dogs were particularly good show specimens but because of his much publicised pack of sealyhams which he hunted as if they were beagles. In addition, he bred a type which he named Lucas terriers: rather like the nineteenth-century sealyham and reputedly good workers. But these met with limited success and few, if any, exist today.

The Rev John Russell

John Russell was born in 1795 at Dartmouth in South Devon, the son of a clergyman who had already gained a reputation as one of the boldest hunters in the county – a title to be inherited by the boy, known as Jack, who was inevitably involved with hounds and terriers from an early age. After leaving Plympton Grammar School to become a pupil at Blundell's School, Tiverton, he did little work and spent all his free hours with some old hounds which he had managed to buy and house with a kindly blacksmith.

When this came to light he was nearly expelled, which evidently gave him a fright because after that he worked hard and won an exhibition that gave him £30 a year for four years. Typically, he spent the first instalment on buying a horse. The man who sold it to him, and incidentally swindled him, was the Rev John Froude of Knowstone on Exmoor, who was to become his friend in later life.

Jack left Tiverton for Exeter College, Oxford, where he read for a degree that would enable him to take holy orders and return to a curacy in Devon. He was ordained in 1820 and accepted the curacy of the village of George Nympton near South Molton, a market town on the edge of Exmoor. He undertook the weekly duty at both the town and the village for a total annual stipend of £60. Though hard to imagine nowadays, this income allowed him to maintain himself and his servants, several horses and a small pack of hounds at George Nympton rectory.

While at Oxford he had bought a terrier bitch named Trump from a milkman, and she was one of his most treasured possessions, 'the perfect terrier'. She may be seen today depicted on the sign of the Jack Russell Inn at Swimbridge, near Barnstaple, a copy reproduced from a painting made during her lifetime. According to her owner the picture was not only a good likeness but showed an example of the best sort of terrier type.

The Rev E. W. L. Davies, Russell's friend, biographer, and one-time curate, never saw Trump alive but describes the original portrait:

> In the first place the colour is white with just a patch of dark tan over each eye and ear, while a similar dot, not larger than a penny piece, marks the root of the tail. The coat, which is thick, close and a trifle wiry, is well calculated to protect the body from wet and cold, but has no affinity with the long, rough jacket of a Scotch terrier. The legs are straight as arrows, the feet perfect; the loins and conformation of the whole frame indicative of hardihood and endurance; while the size and height of the animal may be compared to that of a full-grown vixen fox.

Although Jack Russell favoured white terriers and all his strain were predominantly white, he mated Trump to a black-and-tan dog, probably of the old broken-coated type, and the progeny of these two laid the foundation of the breed that was to bear his name. The choice of sire was an odd one to match with 'the perfect terrier', suggesting that white terriers were not common in Devon in the early 1820s.

Even today opinion is divided on the subject of Parson Jack Russell's principles of terrier breeding. One faction insists that all his dogs were linebred to the bitch Trump, with each pedigree carefully recorded; others hold the view that he was nothing more than a dealer in terriers, buying puppies of good type from farms and reselling them under what now would be described as his brand name. The truth of the matter seems to lie somewhere in between. Years ago I knew two of his relatives, great-nieces who were living near Bideford. One owned a terrier which she and her husband swore was a true descendant of Jack's line; the other dismissed his dog-breeding activities as 'dealing' — by implication a somewhat shady occupation.

In order to understand the way of life enjoyed by Jack Russell and his fellow clerics in the last century it has to be remembered that sons of gentlemen who were not aristocrats with large estates had only three kinds of employment open to them: the Army, the Navy or the church. This explains why a number of country parsons, John Froude among them, had little or no vocation and spent minimum time on pastoral work; they were more interested in archaeology, natural history or hunting.

Russell did take his duties seriously, but they were far from onerous, even when he had charge of two parishes; he was left with plenty of spare time to devote to his hounds and terriers. He kept a small pack at George Nympton and renewed his acquaintance with John Froude, hunting with him and with another disreputable sporting parson named John Radford. The three became known locally as the Black Jacks, which in later years was interpreted to mean that each was as bad as the other, but probably related only to the fact that clergymen out hunting wore black coats instead of scarlet.

This assumption is supported by the fact that Jack Russell was married in 1826 to Miss Penelope Inceldon Bury of Dennington, near Barnstaple; her father was a retired admiral who would have been unlikely to have condoned her marriage to a man of ill-repute. The couple were ideally suited and spent a long and happy life together. She was as keen on hunting as her husband and rode fearlessly to hounds, which in those days was more dangerous for a woman than for a man as she had to ride side-saddle.

Soon after their wedding the Russells moved to the village of Iddesleigh a few miles outside Hatherleigh, where Jack became curate under his father. Here he got together his first real pack of hounds and, because he showed excellent sport and was good-tempered and well-mannered, he was soon invited to draw coverts as far away as Bodmin in Cornwall. Since he took terriers with him as well as hounds, his particular type of terrier became known over a wide area of the English Westcountry, which created a demand for puppies. These sales must have helped to eke out his meagre stipend, which may have tempted him to sell puppies that were not home-bred.

After six years at Iddesleigh, Jack became vicar of Swimbridge and the nearby parish of Landkey, where he and his wife were to remain for nearly fifty years. Here he became renowned as a speaker and for his sermons, and took time off from hunting to support the hospital at Barnstaple and other good works. However, hunting and hounds and terriers remained his abiding interest and these pursuits made him a legend in his own lifetime.

He was a forceful character and to some extent an eccentric, but many of the stories about him which have been handed down over a century or more are apocryphal or relate to John Froude. Some have a ring of truth, such as that of an occasion in Swimbridge church when the lamps failed, preventing him from reading his sermon notes until the sexton had found candles, and he treated his congregation to a discourse on stag hunting.

Rustic poets are still found in Devon, often in village pubs where they are ready to recite their verses to long-suffering tourists in return for pints of beer. In the nineteenth century there were many more to immortalise a local event such as a dramatic hunting day, and Parson Jack's exploits are mentioned in several. This extract is from a collection of fourteen stanzas by an understandably anonymous moorland poet:

But who's that, may I ask, who in grey hue is clad,
Riding wide of the pack, and tight hold of his prad?
'Tis a rare sort of parson, and if there's a run
The Rector of Swymbridge will see all the fun.
His phiz I can't see – by his figure I twigs
It can be no other than Russell on Figs.
If hunting's salvation, he's nothing to fear;
His soul has been hunting for many a year.

But, while he enjoyed a day's stag hunting, his true
enthusiasm lay with his own pack of foxhounds and terriers. The
terriers were gaining wider fame, some being taken abroad by
empire-builders of the time to carry Russell's flag as far as Africa
and India. One of the secrets of his success was that he valued
intelligence as well as stamina.

In those days terriers ran with the hounds and he took pride in
the fact that his dogs knew the country so well that they were
never lost and with some sixth sense could guess where a fox
would run. One of the best known among these clever terriers
was a dog named Tip which would mark where the hounds were
running and then go off on his own, sometimes for several miles,
to be ready at the earth to prevent the hunted fox from going to
ground. Jack disliked 'hard' terriers, meaning dogs that would
attack and fight a fox. 'A real fox terrier,' he said, 'is not meant to
murder, and his intelligence should always keep him from such a
crime.' He claimed that none of his dogs had ever tasted blood:
the terrier's duty was to bay and if possible to bolt a fox.

The first dog show was held in the north of England at
Newcastle-on-Tyne in 1859 and was followed by another event
at Birmingham in the same year. Jack Russell was extremely
critical of show dogs as a whole and fox terriers in particular,
which he said were often produced by crossing a smooth bitch
with an Italian greyhound dog to gain a fine coat, then crossing
the progeny with beagles and bulldogs before selecting from
succeeding litters 'the sires and dams of the modern fox terrier'.
Nevertheless, he took part in numerous shows and, among other
successes, won at the first Bath & West show, held at Exeter in

1862, and judged fox terriers in a show at Bideford the next year.

Within a decade dog shows and show dogs had become popular enough to attract rogues to the game, and it was clear that some form of governing body was essential. The Kennel Club came into being in 1873, with the Rev John Russell as one of its founder members. Its first task was to compile a Stud Book, which was issued the following year, and to formulate rules as guidelines for the future: among these, the committee decided that dogs exhibited at shows not held under Kennel Club rules would be disqualified 'for ever', and this was taken a step further in 1880 when it was laid down that no dog could be exhibited under these rules which was not registered with the Kennel Club.

Jack Russell judged fox terriers at the initial KC show at Crystal Palace, London, in 1874 and remained a member of the club for the rest of his life, though he no longer exhibited his own dogs, preferring to keep a private register of their pedigrees. It is unfortunate for the archivist that a bundle of pedigrees and other papers relating to his terriers which was given to the late Henry Williamson (best known as the author of *Tarka the Otter*) in the 1930s, when he was being encouraged to write a biography, were lost. Admittedly, their interest would be academic after a lapse in time of a century and more, but if nothing else they would prove how many of the parson's dogs were truly linebred to Trump and how many were the product of wheeling and dealing.

Towards the end of his life Jack Russell was offered a living at the village of Black Torrington and the larger annual stipend tempted him to make the move. At the age of eighty-four he still hunted his own small pack of harriers, but he was not happy in his new parish: he was lost without his wife who had died four years earlier and missed old friends around Swimbridge. He kept four terriers in his house, the last he was to own, named Rags, Sly, Fuss and Tinker. Two more and a pair of horses died in a fire that swept through his stables soon after he arrived in the new parish, a disaster which was a great sadness to him, perhaps making him feel that his once happy life was disintegrating.

He died in 1883 and was buried next to his wife in Swimbridge churchyard after a service attended by more than a thousand mourners.

The Kennel Club and breed development

The British Kennel Club and the equivalent organisations in North America and elsewhere are frequently blamed when a breed deteriorates from a working point of view in favour of show points: there is a body of opinion which believes that registration with the KC is a first step on a slippery slope towards poor temperaments, inherited disease and a general lack of stamina. In fact, this is like blaming a computer for issuing inaccurate figures from false information fed to it by a casual operator.

As a rule, what happens is that a group of enthusiasts interested in a hitherto unregistered breed compile a standard of points and submit this to the Kennel Club for recognition, and once this is granted further development on the basis of the standard it is in the hands of breeders and show judges. If the breed then becomes popular, and therefore, in demand, there is a consequent temptation to produce quantity rather than quality – as in the case of miniature poodles bred on puppy farms.

Keen exhibitors know that inbreeding is the quickest means of gaining stardom and if this is not carried out with care and some knowledge of genetics the result can be degeneration in temperament and an increasing incidence of inherited malformation. At one time Irish setters were subject to night blindness and a number of white bullterriers were born deaf, but responsible breeders have eradicated these faults by selective breeding and culling faulty stock. Now several breeds, notably labrador retrievers and alsatians (German shepherds), are suffering from inherited hip dysplasia and progressive retinal atrophy.

Until a few years ago all gundogs (retrievers, pointers, setters and spaniels) which had gained sufficient prizes in the show ring to warrant the title of champion were required to qualify at a field trial to prove that they were obedient, steady to gunfire and capable of performing the type of work expected of the particular breed. The Kennel Club succumbed to pressure from successful exhibitors who were not interested in training dogs to allow two types of champion: a full champion which had passed a field test and a show champion which had not. These are now entered in pedigrees as Ch and Sh Ch, and it has been said that Sh Ch should stand for 'Shame Champion'; there can be little doubt that the KC ruling has not benefited gundogs as a whole.

The effect of the show ring on working terriers has varied, depending on exhibitors' handling techniques and the demands of judges. Wire-haired fox terriers offer an example of one extreme: in order to achieve a sprightly action and to keep the dog 'on its toes', the lead is used to lift it onto the toes of the front feet so that the legs move straight from the shoulder with no flexion of the joints. In the horse world this type of action is described as 'daisy cutting' and is altogether bad, putting a strain on the legs which would lame a dog running any distance over rough ground.

On the other side of the coin, most breeders and exhibitors of Border and Norwich and Norfolk terriers take pains to keep their dogs in working condition, and given the opportunity both cairns and West Highland whites retain the ability to hunt vermin. Irish breeders of the Glen of Imaal terrier go further, insisting that a show dog must gain a *Teastac Misneac*, a certificate proving its gameness against fox or badger, before it can qualify as a champion.

When the British Kennel Club and shows held under its rules came into being in the late 1800s the value of prizewinning dogs soared – in some instances reaching four figures. This meant that terrier breeders were loath to work their dogs for fear of injuries that might mar them for showing and so reduce or even eclipse their potential value; so popular breeds such as fox terriers left the hunting field and were replaced by Jack Russells and other working types.

The Jack Russell Terrier Club wisely allows scarred dogs to compete on equal terms with others provided that such old injuries do not interfere with the ability to work or breed: a torn ear or superficial scars will not prevent a dog from winning in the show ring, but permanent lameness, the loss of an eye or some other crippling defect, will exclude it. If at some time in the future Jack Russells are recognised as a breed by a national kennel club it is to be hoped that this ruling will remain in force to maintain these terriers as a sporting breed.

11

The Jack Russell Terrier Club of Great Britain

The club consists of the national club which governs the constitution, rules and breed standard, and numerous regional clubs which must abide by the rules of the main body but operate with their own committees, administer their own finances and organise shows and other activities within the designated areas.

Regional clubs were formed to encourage more personal contact among members than is possible with one central governing body which may be remote from those living in far corners of Britain, and these have proved very successful. The total membership is now into four figures less than a decade after the club's foundation.

The national club assists the regions in their administration and with finance, and organises one Grand Show a year which travels round Britain to each region in turn.

The regions consist of: South East, South West, Midlands, North Wales, South Wales, Border Counties, North West, Thames Valley, Isle of Wight.

Among affiliated clubs are those in the USA, Australia and Belgium.

Registration

The object of the club's register is to maintain a file on the ancestry of all registered dogs so that the breed can be kept pure and crossbreds rejected. An owner with a purebred Jack Russell may apply to the club for a registration form to enter the puppy in the 'foundation register'. This will require all known details about the animal, including its markings which must be filled in on an outline sketch. This system is similar to that used for the registration of horses, ponies and racing greyhounds.

When application is accepted the owner will receive a registration card bearing a code number and details of the puppy's markings, which will identify it for life. This ensures that a buyer can check by its markings that the puppy on the card is the same animal that is being offered.

Dogs over fifteen months old may qualify for the 'advanced register', but in this case they must be examined and passed by an official inspector before registration. Many owners register a prefix name with the club for a life fee – which at the time of going to press was £3.

Since officials work for the club in an honorary capacity and change from time to time (or move house) the best way for a would-be member to make contact is to attend a terrier show and ask for advice. Applicants from overseas may be able to obtain advice from the Kennel Club, 1 Clarges Street, Piccadilly, London W1Y 8AB. Although the Club has no connection with the JRTCGB, it may know of a breeder who has. Members receive a quarterly magazine which gives news of the club and its regional activities, and publishes articles, letters and advertisements that offer something of interest to all sections of the membership.

The breed standard was drawn up with the main purpose of avoiding physical defects and further introduction of blood from any other breed. The founders of the club are to be congratulated because a boom in the Jack Russell's popularity had put the breed in jeopardy and, before their intervention, it could be said that there were more Jack Russell owners than true Jack Russells.

Two height standards are provided to cover the increasingly popular smaller type of terrier, and allow for the larger dogs preferred by some owners.

144

Breed Standard

Characteristics
The terrier must present a lively, active and alert appearance. It should impress with its fearless and happy disposition. It should be remembered that the Jack Russell is a working terrier and should retain these instincts. Nervousness, cowardice or over-aggression should be discouraged and it should always appear confident.

General Appearance
A sturdy, tough terrier, very much on its toes all the time, measuring between 9in and 15in at the withers. The body length must be in proportion to the height and it should present a compact, balanced image, always being in a solid, hard condition.

Head
Should be well balanced and in proportion to the body. The skull should be flat, of moderate width at the ears, narrowing to the eyes. There should be a defined stop but not over-pronounced. The length of muzzle from the nose to the stop should be slightly shorter than the distance from the stop to the occiput. The nose should be black. The jaw should be powerful and well boned with strongly muscled cheeks.

Eyes
Should be almond shaped, dark in colour and full of life and intelligence.

Ears
Small V-shaped drop ears carried forward close to head and of moderate thickness.

Mouth
Strong teeth with the top slightly overlapping the lower.

(a) Folded ears held slightly out from the head
(b) V-shaped drop ears held close to the cheeks
(c) Pricked ears similar to cairn terrier

Neck

Clean and muscular, of good length, gradually widening at the shoulders.

Forequarters

The shoulders should be sloping and well laid back, fine at points and clearly cut at the withers. Forelegs should be strong and straight-boned with joints in correct alignment. Elbows hanging perpendicular to the body and working free of the sides.

Body

The chest should be shallow, narrow, and the front legs set not too widely apart, giving an athletic, rather than heavily-chested, appearance. As a guide only, the chest should be small enough to be easily spanned behind the shoulders by average-size hands when the terrier is in a fit, working condition. The back should be strong, straight and, in comparison to the height of the terrier, give a balanced image. The loin should be slightly arched.

Hindquarters

Should be strong and muscular, well put together with good angulation and bend of stifle, giving plenty of drive and propulsion. Looking from behind the hocks must be straight.

Feet

Round, hard-padded, of cat-like appearance, neither turning in nor out.

Tail

Should be set rather high, carried gaily and in proportion to body length, usually about 4in long, providing a good hand-hold.

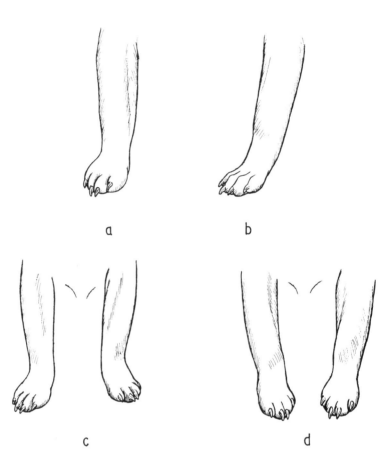

(a) Cat foot – compact, rounded foot suited to digging
(b) Hare foot – long, narrow foot
(c) Front toes turned slightly outwards
(d) Pigeon toes – front feet angled slightly inwards

Coat
Smooth, without being so sparse as not to provide a certain amount of protection from the elements and undergrowth. Rough or broken-coated, without being woolly.

Colour
White should predominate with tan, black or brown markings.

148

Gait

Movement should be free, lively, well co-ordinated with straight action in front and behind.

Note

For showing purposes terriers are classified in two groups: 9in to 12in; over 12in and up to 15in.

Old scars or injuries, the result of work or accident, should not be allowed to prejudice a terrier's chance in the show ring unless they interfere with its movement or with its utility for work or stud.

Male animals should have two apparently normal testicles fully decended into the scrotum.

A Jack Russell terrier should not show any strong characteristics of another breed.

Arthur Heinemann's standard of points

Arthur Heinemann is remembered by Jack Russell terrier breeders because he carried on the original strain, until his death in 1930, from four dogs bequeathed to him by the Rev John Russell, whom he had known since boyhood.

At sometime around the turn of the century Heinemann compiled a standard of points for the Jack Russell terrier, then known as a working fox terrier, based on principles he had learned from Russell himself. He was an odd character; an educated gentleman who not only hunted with hounds, but enjoyed the disreputable 'sport' of badger-digging and baiting with his terriers, which was a pursuit confined to farm workers rather than to his own social peers. However, since he selected and bred his terriers for their gameness against badgers, his strain were tough little dogs of the old type and no doubt some of their descendants remain in the Exmoor area to this day.

Heinemann's standard

Head The skull should be flat, moderately broad, gradually decreasing to the eyes. Little stop should be apparent. The cheeks must not be full. Ears V-shaped and small, of moderate thickness and dropping forward close to the cheek, not by the side. Upper and lower jaws strong and muscular and of fair punishing strength. Not much falling away below the eyes. The nose should be black. The eyes dark, small and deep set, full of fire, life, and intelligence and circular in shape. Teeth level, upper on the outside of the lower.

Neck Clean and muscular, of fair length, gradually widening to shoulders.

Shoulders Long and sloping, well laid back, fine at points, clearly cut at withers.

Chest Deep but not broad.

Back Straight and strong with no appearance of slackness.

Loins Powerful, very slightly arched, fore ribs moderately arched, back ribs deep. The terrier should be well ribbed up.

Hindquarters Strong and muscular, free from droop, thighs long and powerful, hocks near the ground, dog standing well upon them. Not straight in the stifle.

Stern Set on high, carried gaily but never over back or curled. Of good strength and length. A 'pipe-cleaning' tail or too short is most objectionable.

Legs Perfectly straight, showing no ankle in front. Strong in bone throughout, short and straight forward when travelling, stifles not turned outward. Elbows should hang perpendicular to the body, working free to the side.

Feet Round, compact, not large, soles hard and tough, toes moderately arched, turned neither in nor out.

Coat Dense, a trifle wiry, abundant. Belly and underside of thighs not bare.

Colour White with acceptable tan, grey or black at head and root of rail. Red, brindle or liver marks are objectionable.

Symmetry, size and character Terrier must present a gay, lively and active appearance. Bone and strength in a small compass are essentials, but not cloggy or coarse. Speed and endurance must be apparent. Not too short or too long in leg. Fourteen inches to withers the ideal for a dog, thirteen for a bitch. Weight when in working condition about fourteen pounds but a pound more or less entirely acceptable. Conformation that of an adult vixen.

Disqualifying points Too short, too leggy, legs not straight, nose white, cherry or spotted considerably with these colours. Ears Prick, Tulip or Rose. Mouth under or over shot. Excessively nervous or savage.

Glossary of Terms

Action The movement when walking or trotting.

Apple head A rounded skull. A fault.

Bat-eared With pricked ears. A fault.

Blaze Strip of white hair running from the nose up between the eyes.

Bloom Gloss on a healthy coat.

Bolt To force a hunted animal out of hiding.

Bone 'Having good bone' describes a strongly but not coarsely-built dog.

Brace Two well-matched dogs.

Brisket Chest between the forelegs.

Butterfly nose With flesh-coloured markings on the nose. A fault.

Cat feet Rounded, compact feet.

Chest The body between the brisket and belly.

Cow-hocked Having hocks turned inwards towards each other instead of being parallel. A fault.

Croup Area immediately behind the root of the tail.

Dam Female parent.

Dewclaws Supernumerary claws found on the inside of the front legs. Occasionally on the hind legs of terriers of mixed ancestry.

Docking Surgical shortening of the tail.

Drop-ears Pendant ears, hanging close to the face.

Elbow Joint at the top of the foreleg; being 'out at elbows' is a fault.

Estrus Used in the USA for *Oestrus.*

Gunshy A dog that is frightened by gunfire, due either to lack of sympathetic training or (more rarely) abnormally acute hearing.

Hare feet Long narrow feet with spread toes. A fault.

Haw Inner eyelid (*Membrana nictitans*).

Heat Term for oestrus or 'season' in bitches.

Hocks Joints in the hind legs, equivalent to the ankles in man.

Hound-marked Having coloured patches similar to the markings on foxhounds and beagles; usually applies to tricolours.

Kennel Club Governing body of the British canine world, excluding Jack Russell terriers and racing greyhounds.

Knee Joint in the front leg. Incorrectly used as this joint is the equivalent of our wrist.

Leggy Too long in the leg. A fault.

Level jaw Teeth meet correctly.

Mask The foreface.

Oestrus Period when bitches are ready to mate. Usually occurs twice annually.

Pastern Lower section of the leg, below the knee in the forelegs and below the hock in the hindlegs.

Pig jaw Over-shot jaw. A fault.

Prefix Kennel name granted by Jack Russell Terrier Club. This forename is then applied to all dogs bred by the owner.

Prick-eared With ears carried erect, like those of a Welsh corgi. A fault.

Ring-tailed Having a tail that curls over the back. A fault.

Shoulder The top of the shoulder blade.

Sire Male parent.

Snipy Having a muzzle that is too long and narrow. A fault.

Stifle The first joint below the hip.

Tight-lipped Having the correct form of lips for a Jack Russell. Loose lips, resembling a spaniel's, are a fault.

Tricolour White dog with black and tan markings. See Hound-marked.

Unsound Having a fault in structure or health which renders the dog useless for work, show, etc.

Variety meats American term for offal.

Varmint Old English for a fierce little terrier prepared to tackle any adversary. Generally such animals are unsuitable as companion dogs.

Vixen Female fox.

Whelping Giving birth to puppies.

Acknowledgements

My grateful thanks to all those members of the Jack Russell Terrier Club of Great Britain who have loaned photographs to illustrate this book: Ann Brewer, Thelma Loomes, Brian Male, Mary Shannon, Roma Spencer, E. A. Rawlinson, Peter and Caroline Wheatland, Ruth Hussey Wilford, and the Vicar and Churchwardens of Swimbridge PPC, Devon.

Thanks also to Tom Horner of *Dog World*, Vernon Bartlett and Fred Swannell, for their valuable advice.

Index